SO YOU V ⌐E

A

LORRY DRIVER?

KEVIN J MERVIN

A wanna be truckers rough guide and some nostalgia for old farts that have been there, done it, got the T-shirt

In larger print to suit the trade we love to hate

Published by

Foot in the Door Publishing

All rights reserved

First Edition published 2021

© remains with the author

A catalogue record for this book is available from the British Library

Other books by Kevin J Mervin

Weekend Warrior: A Territorial Soldier's war in Iraq

PTSD: Living Comfortably Numb

Millennials: OMG! Like so offended right now

Acknowledgement
Preface
Introduction

Acknowledgement

I would like to take this opportunity to thank the British Army, in particular my old trade bosses in the Royal Electrical Mechanical Engineers (REME), arranging and paying for my HGV Category C+E course so I may continue my course and qualify to become a Recovery Mechanic – best trade in the army. And thank you RAF for lending one of your examiners to the army for the day and having confidence in my driving ability. In particularly negotiating the narrow streets of Abingdon in your 6-speed Ford Cargo articulated vehicle with a single axle 30-feet trailer.

As for the many driving agencies I had the misfortune to gain shaky and shady assignments of suspicious so-called full time employment, I certainly do not thank for giving me terrible work full time employed drivers would not touch with a barge pole. And not forgetting transport clerks giving me grief during my agency driving career, abusing and using agency drivers as scapegoats to cover-up these ill-educated arses for all the catastrophes made with almost all delivery runs. Oh, and for trying to walk upright. Give it up folks, you're fighting a losing battle.

Last but not least I have to mention the former European Union (EU) for having an incredible ignorant misunderstanding of HGV's and making the haulage industry in the United Kingdom (UK) outrageously expensive for drivers to sustain a vocational licence. Hauliers alike, having to comply with pathetic rules, laws, directives and regulations that constantly make it more and more difficult to deliver goods whilst keeping commerce, businesses, even entire countries to run smoothly.

Preface

In 1861 Nikolaus August Otto invented and patented the first two-stroke internal combustion engine. By 1885, Karl Benz, another German engineer, designed, constructed and patented the first horseless vehicle – a tricycle – powered by his own internal combustion engine. In the same year two other German engineers, Gottlieb Daimler and his business partner Wilhelm Maybach, designed and built a horseless carriage, again, using a tricycle construction. Just over a decade later Wilhelm Maybach designed and built the first internal combustion engine powered heavy goods vehicle – the Heavy Goods Vehicle (HGV) was born.

Adapting and refining his design to become more efficient than steam power, Rudolf Diesel, another important inventor of future truck design, built the first, yet crude, diesel engine in 1893. Since, truck manufactures have come and gone the world over. Each leaving a legacy of huge leaps in technology for the next generation of engineers to improve upon and manufacture trucks with the capability of moving huge loads Maybach could only dream of.

From the very start British steam powered truck manufactures, inspired by Maybach and Diesel, quickly realised the potential of their inventions and developed bigger and better trucks with better gearboxes, wheels, axles, and the ability to carry heavier loads over longer distances.

The haulage business soon became a massive worldwide industry, designing and manufacturing more and more HGV's to thunder down our highways, creating a need for better motorway networks. And because more trucks used public roads governments were quick to realise HGV's needed categorising depending on size and load carrying capabilities. Vocational licences were soon introduced, along with driver training and tests.

From Maybach in the late 19th Century to Mercedes in the 21st Century, never has an industry seen so much change in such a small space of time: disc brakes, Exhaust Gas Re-circulation (EGR) valves, variable pitch turbo chargers, Advance Braking System (ABS), Electronic Braking System (EBS), lane departure warning cameras, catalytic converters, Diesel Particulate Filter (DPF) chemical factory exhaust systems, plus many other efficiency and safety assemblies used in modern cars were first developed for trucks. And new ideas are continuously researched in driver and pedestrian safety systems, fuel efficiency and automotive environmental development, including fully autonomous vehicles. Training, licences, driver disciplines, even politics has contributed towards the modern and future heavy haulage industry.

Introduction

If you are thinking of becoming a lorry driver, please, please, please, think long and hard about this particular hazardous career move. It is an extremely stressful, thankless and unappreciated job. Having to work long unsociable hours, only to eventually return home physically and mentally knackered, wreaking of sweaty cab odour, and develop sleep apnoea. You also have to adhere to an unbelievable wedge of bureaucratic nonsense – EU driving directives as well as UK regulations. Oh, not forgetting them – cyclists.

To rub salt into the somewhat disillusioned romantic wound of becoming King of the open road, it is ludicrously expensive to become a HGV driver, having to take 3 other driving tests before reaching HGV category, outrageously expensive to retain a vocational licence, and you have yet to earn a single penny. However, if you are determined to become a truck driver, or just curious about the trucking world, I hope you learn something from my book. Maybe take away with you a piece of advice or a snippet of information that you had previously placed upon the parcel shelf of yesteryear.

Kevin J Mervin, author of Weekend Warrior: A Territorial soldier's war in Iraq, PTSD: Living comfortably numb, and Millennials: OMG! Like so offended right now, has written another book reflecting a subject he clearly understands and recognises. With a shed-load of various HGV skills he has collated over the past 37-years working within the industry, Kevin shares his knowledge and wealth of experience with hope of dissuading those from having a foolish desire of becoming a HGV driver.

Kevin's automotive career started in 1984 working for Cummins Diesel, a division of Cummins Engine Company, employed as a parts sales advisor, supplying engine parts to the workshop and trade customers. After a few years he moved to a different part of the UK to work for a Seddon Atkinson dealership employed as a parts advisor. Here he learnt many aspects of the industry, including other trucks such as ERF and Foden, where 'Common Parts' were shared between the big three British truck manufactures.

In 1995 he joined his local Territorial Army (TA) unit where he trained as a heavy recovery mechanic using the 6X4 20-tonne Leyland-Scammell Eka and the 6X6 27-tonne Foden Eka recovery vehicle. In 1999 and after being made redundant – twice – he worked for a company that repaired car transporters and trailers as well as rigid and articulated trucks. Employed to create a parts department, Kevin also got his hands dirty in the workshop with repairs, inspections and servicing.

In March 2003 Kevin was called-out by HM Government to fight in Iraq, attached to the Royal Tank Regiment. Upon his return home, and due to circumstances beyond his control, Kevin was left with no alternative but use his HGV licence and sign up to several driving agencies and earn a crust whilst searching for a full time job. During his agency days (or rather nights) Kevin quickly experienced their empty promises and lack of support. Nevertheless, after many assignments with different haulage companies and operators he gained further experience with different truck variants – new and old – adding yet more strings to his HGV bow.

Kevin also has an interest in history, including trucks, and by mixing his ingredients of automotive knowledge created this book, from birth of HGV's to the concept of fully autonomous trucks in the 21st Century. Painting a true account of why it is an incredibly bad idea becoming a truck driver, including the outrageously expensive driving tests, the introduction of compulsory digi-cards, the EU derived Driver Certificate of Professional Competence card (DCPC) drivers need – at their own expense – to the incredibly intrusive and complicated EU rules, laws, directives and regulations created over the decades that have made it virtually impossible for haulage companies, operators and drivers to adhere to.

Chapter 1

GENESIS

In the good old days, by which I mean pre-1996, being a lorry driver was almost an enjoyment. And yes, many will say 1996 was nowhere near as good as 1986, 1976 or 1966, and so on. So when was the real, genuine golden era for truckers, and where did it all start? Well, the beginning is a good place to start, and that was during the latter part of the 19th Century. To be a little more accurate the innovation of self-propelled internal combustion engine powered trucks begun in 1896.

Born in Germany, the original purpose-built truck powered by a recently invented internal combustion engine was soon adapted, improved and re-designed by brilliant innovative British inventors and engineers. Oh, not forgetting a gaggle of Americans and a Canadian thrown in for good measure, becoming the most important contributors to truck manufacturing. So to start the ball rolling, or rather the truck moving, an engine is required. And thanks to Nikolaus August Otto, in 1861 he invented and patented the first two-stroke internal combustion engine that ran on gas as its fuel.

Otto and his business partner, Eugen Langen – a German industrialist – realised its potential and hastily built a factory to develop further models and improve performance, rewarded with a gold medal at the World Fair for their

efforts. Spurred on by his success, Otto went on to develop a more powerful four-stroke internal combustion engine, becoming the first reliable replacement for the clumbersum steam engine.

Karl Benz, another German engineer, designed, constructed and patented the first horseless vehicle – a tricycle – powered by his own internal combustion engine in 1885. In the same year, however, two other German engineers, Gottlieb Daimler and his business partner Wilhelm Maybach, designed and built a horseless carriage, again using a tricycle construction. They also designed a new engine – the Daimler-Maybach engine. Lighter and smaller than Otto's design, it included a revolutionary fuel injection carburettor.

The following year Daimler improved his tricycle by using one of Wilhelm Wimpff & Son's stagecoaches, adapting it to allow Daimler's own engine to fit in its chassis. It was this particular design of vehicle that became the true world first four-wheeled horseless carriage powered by an internal combustion engine. The car was born. Three years later Daimler and Maybach designed and improved another four-wheeled vehicle from scratch, fitted with their own engine, chassis, body and gearbox – a four-speed transmission giving the car a top speed of a whopping 10 mph.

Wilhelm Maybach, a name associated with 21st Century luxury car design, was actually the pioneer of internal combustion engine powered trucks. Maybach's other brilliant inventions include the gearwheel transmission in 1889 and the float-chamber spray-jet carburettor in 1893. He also developed a more efficient cooling system by designing a honeycombed core radiator, revolutionising all modern radiators used today.

In 1896, whilst working for Gottlieb Daimler, Maybach designed the first purpose-built truck powered by a 4 horse powered (hp) engine and a gearbox with two forward and one reverse gears. Interest, however, in his load-carrying contraption didn't impress the German folk at all, but he didn't give up hope. Maybach was convinced his invention will one day not only supersede horse-drawn carts and steam powered wagons, but also carry bigger and heavier loads over long distances without the need for constant refuelling on the way.

Eleven years later, and almost seven years after Gottlieb died, Maybach resigned from Gottlieb Daimler's company, Motoren Gesellschaft, to pursue his interest in designing better, more efficient trucks. In 1909, after inventing the incredibly powerful, yet immense 120hp overhead valve twin-ignition engine, he started his own company.

Maybach's new designs still failed to convince a suspicious German market that his horseless goods wagon was the way forward. To any potential customer it was nothing more than an under-powered cart that struggled to pull a payload of only 1.5 tons. Needless to say it was a frustrating time for Maybach, especially when this incredibly brilliant engineer spent so much of it designing an innovative coil spring suspension system at the rear to accompany a transverse mounted elliptical leaf spring suspension system at the front. This new concept of his suspension design was developed to cope with the terrible pot-holed dirt roads and dampen the vibration caused by the engine (anti-vibration engine mounts were yet to be invented).

The 1.6 litre 4hp two-cylinder engine mounted to the rear of the truck was originally developed by Gottlieb Daimler for a car chassis fuelled by various flammables such as gas from coal, recently refined petroleum, and even lamp oil. The truck variant, however, could only run on petroleum so to supply the engine its optimum power output. And petrol was bought only from chemists, because the humble rip-off service station was yet to be invented.

Drive belts transmitted the engine power to a shaft fitted with pinions at both ends mounted transversely to the vehicle's longitudinal axis. Each of these pinions meshed with a ring gear connected to one of the rear wheels acting as the drive wheel. And yet, with all his engineering innovations, improvements and tweaking, still no sales.

Maybach eventually found a buyer for his truck in England after tests were undertaken in Liverpool to see if it could actually replace steam powered wagons that had been improved, tried and tested. But there was one small problem. Up until 1896 steam powered traction engines were restricted to no more than 4mph – fast walking speed – and had to carry a crew of three: two for operating the vehicle and one to walk ahead waving a red flag warning other road users of their approach. In particular horse-drawn carts so not to startle the horses and crash into a ditch. But speed wasn't the issue; power was, and the ability to transport heavy loads.

By the beginning of the 20th Century the incredible momentum of vehicle technology, coupled with the inevitable need for speed, it became apparent goods and individuals could get from A to B quicker without the need of someone walking and waving a red flag in front of them. So sod the horse. Maybach took advantage of the abolishment, much to the disappointed of horse-drawn cart operators, by designing a faster truck that carried heavier payloads of up to an incredible 5-tons. Thanks to predicted sales and excitement from his best customer, England, truck improvements soon paid dividends.

Maybach's first truck, with an engine capacity of 4hp and the ability to carry a payload of only 1.5-tons, was soon adapted to carry a maximum of 5-tons by increasing the engine's power output to an amazing 10hp. Maybach also re-designed the chassis by moving the engine to the front whilst fitting a 4-speed gearbox towards the rear for proportionate weight distribution. And modern car manufacturers thought they pioneered 50/50 chassis balancing.

Within the same year Maybach built a further four models. Meanwhile, in England, the concept of using an internal combustion engine powered truck was well and truly established. And in 1897 further improvements were quickly adapted to entice further sales in the UK including better performance and the ability to carry heavier payloads.

The engine established its position by remaining towards the front of the vehicle with a propshaft connecting to a gearbox at the rear, transferring power to a differential at the axle. The glow-tube ignition system fitted to earlier engines was replaced with a low-voltage magneto system designed by Bosch that ignited petrol in the improved 2.2 litre engine.

And these many improvements were tantamount of becoming a completely new truck design, incorporating a recently developed coolant system and the innovative tubular radiator with a honeycombed core. But remarkably wheels remained the same. No different to a horse-drawn wagon design — a steel cladded wooden structure with wooden spokes.

Even though Maybach improved the load carrying truck and created sales in England, potential German customers remained stubborn and unconvinced of its ability to transport goods. It was arrogantly assumed that his new contraption vehicle was best left to horse-drawn carts, refusing to accept internal combustion could ever supersede steam power. A cogent paradigm would be a GPS satellite navigation aid being invented during the pinnacle of paper folded map technology. Clever gadget, but will never catch on.

Meanwhile, back in England, Maybach certainly won the hearts and minds of steam powered truck operators, and most definitely inspired existing manufactures such as the Lancashire Steam Motor Company based in Leyland, created by James Sumner and Henry Spurrier in 1896. And in 1904 they too had built their own internal combustion petrol engine powered truck. Three years later the company incorporated into their business the steam wagon builder, Coulthards of Preston, becoming the more recognisable Leyland Motors Limited.

Leyland: The newly formed company developed and manufactured their first petrol powered 3-ton truck for the military, becoming the British Army standard utility vehicle. Production started in 1913 at their Farington plant, and by the time soldiers were digging the first trenches in 1914 the company employed 1,500 staff, producing over 1,200 petrol-powered trucks and over 400 steam-powered wagons.

The outbreak of World War One had a huge effect on Leyland Motors Limited. At its peak the company doubled its staff to just over 3,000 producing almost 6,000 vehicles for the British Army and Auxillary Forces alone. After the war Leyland bought Kingston-upon-Thames former aircraft factory when commissioned by the government to recondition a surplus stock of 3,000 ex-military 3-ton Leyland trucks.

The British government, now skint from the war and desperate for cash, set about raising funds to support the needs of the nation. One particular project was to recondition trucks used in the war and sell to any civilian customer who wanted to use them for whatever reason. Leyland Motors Limited had other ideas and actually purchased the lot, if only to stop them filtering into the civilian market and tarnishing Leyland's reputation for quality. By doing so, Leyland could sell them to customers that fully understood how to operate their trucks.

By the early 1920's Leyland Motors Limited became the forefront of truck design, naming their products after majestic animals such as the Lion, Tiger, Bison and Buffalo. Other trucks such as Titan, Titanic and the Leviathon were also developed to attract customers, where some of these names are still recognised today, such as the Terrier.

Leyland Motors Limited continued to develop large trucks including the Hippo and Rhino, accompanying their smaller range such as the Cub, which oddly replaced the Trojan. The following decade Leyland realised diesel power was the way forward, and even developed their own compression ignition engine, consequently kick-starting the demise of petrol engines fitted into trucks, and most definitely steam powered road locomotion.

Foden: Another British truck builder aware of Maybach's incredible leap forward in truck design, and its huge potential in load carrying, was Edwin Richard Foden. Edwin started as an apprentice for an agricultural engineering company, Plant & Hancock, of Sandbach, Cheshire, designing and manufacturing industrial and agricultural traction engines. When George Hancock retired, Edwin bought the company, re-naming it Edwin Foden & Sons.

In 1881 Edwin built his first traction engine and by 1898 pioneered the fitting of steel wheels to his steam powered wagons. It wasn't until 1913 when vulcanised solid rubber tyres were introduced, Edwin continued his wheel pioneering technology by developing them to be the first pneumatic tyre fitted to trucks. And because of the pneumatic tyre he was able to design and manufacture a purpose built 8-ton truck powered by the new Gardner lightweight (LW), high-speed oil engine.

By the latter part of the 1920's Edwin realised the potential of diesel power reliability, efficiency and economy well before Leyland. But the board of directors failed to recognise this, so Edwin and his son, Dennis, retired from the board. Edwin and Dennis, however, carried on truck manufacturing, and with a much needed cash injection from the family created a new company called ERF (initials of

Edwin Richard Foden) to develop and manufacture diesel powered trucks.

Edwin Foden & Sons continued designing and manufacturing steam powered trucks, later realising Edwin was correct about diesel power, and although a little later than Leyland and Edwin, by the early 1940's re-introduced some much-improved models. A decade later they designed a rear engine mounted truck and developed a lightweight glass reinforced plastic cab – synonymous to Foden trucks today – leading to the development of the first tilt cab design in 1962.

In 1964 Edwin Foden & Sons designed a vehicle to compete with the 32-ton market. But in 1974 the company faced harsh financial difficulties and needed the government to intervene with a huge cash injection, which they did by creating military contracts, giving the company a huge reprieve so to continue its recovery. But it wasn't enough. By 1980 Edwin Foden & Sons hit further financial difficulties and the British government were not prepared to bail out the company a second time.

Edwin Foden & Sons had no alternative but sell up, luckily finding an American truck manufacturer, PACCAR in 1996 who also bought the Dutch truck manufacturer DAF and Leyland Trucks in 1998 re-naming it Leyland-DAF. Edwin Foden & Sons trucks were now re-badged using a range of DAF trucks – namely the DAF 95 cab – with the Foden name, if only to appease the British truck industry and its loyal customers. But in 2006 PACCAR had no choice but dump the re-badged Foden, leaving them to concentrate on the highly successful DAF range of trucks.

ERF: With a little help from Edwin Richard Foden, his son Dennis and two former colleagues, including chief engineer Ernest Sherratt, created their first truck in 1933 fitted with a Gardner diesel. The chassis number was 63 – Edwin Foden's age. E. R. Foden & Son insisted on the best and continued to use Gardner engines, David Brown gearboxes, Kirkstall Forge axles and Sandbach coach builder, John Henry Jennings, providing his factory to assemble the vehicles. The 63 chassis numbered truck, designated with the model C.I (Compression Ignition), was displayed at the motor show in Olympia. The rest of the chassis number included the number of cylinders followed by the number of wheels.

ERF trucks soon gained interest from haulage companies. However, by 1939 and increased tension with Nazi Germany, Gardner prioritised engine production for military vehicles. In the meantime ERF needed to build trucks for the war effort so an additional engine supplier had to be found to keep up with demand. AEC came to their rescue with a 7.7 litre engine, using a distinct identification of D.I incorporated into the chassis number so to differentiate identification from Gardner powered trucks.

ERF became an established and trusted truck manufacturer by the end of World War Two, and in 1948 introduced a new style of cab built by John Henry Jennings, naming it the V Type. Following the death of Edwin Foden in 1950 Dennis became managing director at the age of only 36-years. And in 1956 he introduced Rolls Royce diesel engines to his range of vehicles.

Dennis Foden unfortunately died in 1960 leaving ERF to his brother Peter taking the reins, and he quickly made changes. In 1961 the Cummins diesel engine was introduced to power ERF eight wheeler chassis with their KV model cab, first selling the American powered units to haulier Charles Butt of Northampton. In later years Perkins diesel engines were also added to the options list, but Gardner engines continued to domineer the ERF truck range. Introduction of Cummins engines, however, with its reliability, efficiency and economy, quickly rivalled competition from other engine manufacturers and took the lead in power domination.

Peter continued his changes, one of which was to introduce the revolutionary Long Vue (LV) cab, making its debut appearance at the Earls Court Commercial Motor Show, fitted to ERF distributor Frank Tucker's eight wheel tipper. And by the late 1960's managed to poach Eric Green from Atkinson trucks and Alan Turner from Chrysler Dodge to design new vehicles and stay competitive. Soon afterwards they developed the 'A' Series. A lighter yet strong chassis with new split cross members, longer outboard mounted rear springs, rear axle shock absorbers and an innovation of condensing various parts and assemblies.

The 'A' Series, manufactured only as a tractor unit, became a success and catapulted ERF to a record overall sales total of 9.7 million units, until the introduction of the 'B' Series in 1974. Thanks to a huge success of the 'A' Series, in 1970 ERF wanted to purchase struggling British truck builder Atkinson. But it wasn't to be. Instead, the sale surprisingly went to Seddon, thus becoming Seddon Atkinson, using similar major components as ERF including Cummins, Gardner and Rolls Royce diesel engines, Eaton/Fuller gearboxes and Rockwell axles.

By the early 1980's British truck manufactures faced uncertainty due to a serious decline in sales, exacerbated by a national recession and cheaper foreign imports. Even the global success of ERF wasn't immune. The economic downturn had a massive effect on the company's production, dramatically falling to only 16 units manufactured per week.

By 1983 employees fell from 1,400 to around 600 but incredibly ERF managed to struggle through thanks to a new innovative idea introduced to streamline the business: 'CP' (Common Parts) Series. An idea that became popular with customers simply because parts were readily available. And the new parts procurement system also benefited from sales for Foden and Seddon Atkinson sharing many components with ERF production line requirements, simultaneously producing further sales within the shared parts family tree.

In 1988 the new 'CP' Series exceeded sales predictions and ERF quickly took advantage by introducing the 'E' Series tractor unit with a new SP4 cab, selling over 3,500 units in the UK alone. During this time ERF signed a partnership deal with the Austrian truck manufacturer Steyr, using their cabs for the ES6 & ES8 vehicle range. After a £14 million investment, in 1993 ERF added the 'EC' Series to their incredible portfolio, becoming their most successful truck in its entire history.

However, in typical British industrial fashion, when a company is doing well and showing a good profit, share holders and boardroom directors, with no morals or pride, became greedy. In 1996 ERF was sold to Western Star Trucks, British Columbia, where two models still carrying the ERF name were introduced to the municipal market – EM and EU Series. Inevitably, the new yet unstable ownership didn't last. Four years later Western Star Trucks sold ERF to the German truck manufacturer MAN. And within the same year two further models were launched – ECS and ECX Series.

MAN built a new factory in Middlewich, Cheshire, not far from the original home of ERF at Sandbach, costing around £28 million, to develop and produce the new ERF range. But the investment plans to secure a future for ERF wasn't to be. In 2002 MAN pulled the plug fearing further losses whilst concentrating on additional expensive investments around the globe. ERF had no option but accept the fact MAN was no longer interested in the British truck manufacturer, putting to rest yet another UK truck manufacturer with one stroke of a pen.

Scammell: One of the most important pioneering British truck manufactures began its debut in the early 1900's. The London based company based in Spitalfields, established by Wheelwright George Scammell, named the company G. Scammell & Nephew. They started the fledgling company building and repairing carts, and within a few years sold and maintained Foden steam-powered wagons.

Edward Rudd, a customer of George Scammell, bought a Knox tractor in the USA and shipped it over to the UK. Impressed with the payload he asked George to have a look and see if he could build a vehicle similar to the Knox tractor, believing there were a huge market. G. Scammell & Nephew made some improvements and by the beginning of the First World War made rapid changes with designs and innovations to meet demands for the war effort.

George's great nephew, Lieutenant Colonel Alfred George, fought in the First World War. Unfortunately he was injured and hastily evacuated back to Blighty, only to be discharged from service due to his injuries. But during his deployment in France he learnt the benefit of trailer articulation and was eager to adapt it to civilian vehicles. Within a few years after the war G. Scammell & Nephew designed the articulated Scammell 6-wheeler, capable of carrying a payload of 7.5-tons and with a top speed of 12 mph. Further improvements were made, managing 18mph whilst carrying 8-tons.

With its amazing test results it wasn't long before customers placed orders and G. Scammell & Nephew needed larger premises to cope with demand, moving to Tolpits Lane, Watford, Hertfordshire. Later the same year the company re-named itself to Scammell Lorries Ltd., with Alfred acting as the Managing Director. Success of the Scammell articulated 6-wheeler unit allowed the company to develop carriers and trailers for it to pull, where one of its many happy customers was Shell-Mex, leading to a bespoke design of a frameless tanker in 1926.

The following year Scammell pioneered the market for off-road large vehicles with introduction of The Pioneer. A new design with a 6x4 rigid chassis, driven front axle and a walking-beam bogie so its wheels could raise 2-feet without losing traction. A 6X6 configuration rigid chassis was also developed. By 1929 Scammell, confident in their off-road design capability, developed a 100-ton vehicle – the largest articulated truck ever built. Only two were ever made, fitted with the Scammell 7ltr petrol engine, consuming 1-gallon per ¾ mile.

Two years later, realising diesel engines offered better power and economy, Scammell fitted a Gardner 6LW engine with a massive improvement in fuel consumption of 4.2 mpg. Whilst carrying out further tests using diesel power, the 100-ton payload was also dramatically improved, capable of pulling 165 tons. In 1933 Scammell, with designer Oliver North, created and developed a new automatic coupling, enabling the unit and trailer to turn in less than its own length. The Scammell 8-wheeler, fitted with a 6-speed gearbox designed by Oliver North, was again powered by the Gardner 6LW. But these particular trucks were expensive, and like other manufacturers during the 1930's the great depression took a damaging effect on the company.

Scammell Lorries Ltd., miraculously survived and in 1937 developed new innovative designs including the forward-control rigid 8-wheeler. By the Second World War Scammell, like other manufacturers, became a huge contributor to the war effort. Supply of vehicles to the military included tank transporters, gun tractors and heavy recovery vehicles. After the war, and by no means forgetting Her Majesty's Armed Forces by any means, Scammell continued to supply the 6x6 Explorer, 4x4 Mountaineer and Constructor vehicles. The company also diversified its heavy vehicle range towards construction and engineering industries including mining, logging and oil companies.

By the 1950's Scammell heavy off-road vehicles were fitted with Rolls Royce diesel engines – the C6 turbo charged engine – and a semi-automatic gearbox. In 1955 Scammell became a member of the Leyland Group, fitting their engines to lighter vehicles such as the Scammell 4x2 Highwayman motive unit and the forward control Routeman 8-wheeler.

It didn't take long for Scammell to recognise the power and economy of Cummins diesel engines, and in 1964 fitted the first Cummins N Series 335 into their 6X4 Contractor, with a Lipe clutch and Fuller gearbox. The Contractor found success as a heavy haulage vehicle, becoming the British army prime tank transporter with the optional 30/40-ton and Leyland 24-ton bogies.

In 1969 the 6X4 Crusader was introduced, which was also developed for the military, including a recovery vehicle variant powered by a Rolls Royce 305 engine. A 4X2 variant was produced for BRS (British Road Services) fitted with Rolls Royce 220 and 280 diesel engines. Becoming a member of the Leyland Group resulted in a further name change to Scammell Motors, and by the mid 1970's built the Contractor Mk2 fitted with a huge Cummins 18-ltr K Series engine developing 450bhp, driven by an Allison automatic gearbox.

A military variant was introduced in 1983 operated as a tank transporter, with a 100-ton pull capability. Powered by the 26-ltr Rolls Royce CV12TCE dual-turbo charged 625bhp V12 diesel engine, it was accompanied by a semi-automatic gearbox and a Scammell 40-ton bogie. It also had a new cab, braking and winching system developed to cope with heavier loads.

By the 1980's Leyland Group, with Scammell, developed an 8-wheeler Constructor, adopting the much needed modern Leyland tilt cab for further development on future trucks – 4X2, 6X2 and 6X4 S26 Series tractor units, replacing the Crusader A Series. S26 being fitted with a range of gearboxes, engines and axles from the S24 for various application use.

British army received a 6x6 version in 1986 fitted with a Rolls-Royce Eagle 350 engine driven by a ZF automatic gearbox. Scammell also supplied an 8x6 hooklift DROPS variant, winning a tender to supply 1,522 units. Leyland Group, however, was bought out by the Dutch truck manufacturer, DAF BV, becoming the supplier of DROPS military specification variant, and closed the Scammell factory for good in July 1988.

Seddon Atkinson: Atkinson & Co. were founded in Preston, Lancashire, by brothers Edward Atkinson, Henry Birch Atkinson and brother-in-law George Hunt. Edward Atkinson started in business as a Millwright in 1907 and went on to repairing steam powered trucks. As the business grew Edward designed and produced his own steam powered wagons. But Edward Atkinson filed for bankruptcy in 1931 and 3-years later a new truck company miraculously appeared: Atkinson Lorries. Within a few years the newly formed truck manufacturer built their first diesel trucks powered by a Gardner.

Returning from the First World War, Herbert and Robert Seddon started a new business in 1919 with Ernest Foster importing trucks. By the late 1930s Foster and Seddon Ltd., built their own diesel engine powered vehicles, and were first to fit Perkins diesel engines manufactured by Frank Perkins Ltd., as original equipment. When the Second World War interrupted production both Seddon and Atkinson managed to produce vehicles for civilian use along with vehicles for the war effort, including Seddon manufacturing trailers for the Ministry of Supply.

Seddon moved to Oldham in 1948 taking over the Woodstock Mill – previously used to produce Rolls Royce engine parts for Spitfires – and concentrate on lighter truck market designs. At the same time Atkinson Lorries moved to their Walton-le-Dale site at Preston to develop trucks for the heavier market. And in 1970 Seddon surprised many bidders, including ERF, to win the takeover of Atkinson Lorries.

Seddon Atkinson Vehicles Ltd. was born on 1st January 1971, continuing their vehicle production at their individual sites. And yet again, in typical British industrial fashion, was sold 3-years later to International Harvester, USA. However, IH invested in the company rather than turn around a quick profit to sell again as soon as possible. In 1975 Seddon Atkinson developed the 400 Series tractor unit, built at both plants. But in 1980 the national recession started and quickly hit many manufactures, including the building trade, where Seddon Atkinson supplied many vehicles to building manufactures.

Further bad news followed, if not predicted, with International Harvester withdrawing from Europe and selling Seddon Atkinson Vehicles to ENASA owned by the nationalised Pegaso Company, Spain, in 1984. ENASA launched with Seddon Atkinson the Strato range in 1988, with a Seddon Atkinson chassis fitted with a Pegaso cab, produced in Madrid, Spain.

The following year saw yet another buy-out bidding frenzy between MAN, Daimler-Benz and Fiat; the latter succeeding and buying Pegaso 1st January 1991 becoming part of the IVECO Group, the commercial vehicle division of Fiat. Seddon Atkinson went on to produce a wide range of commercial and municipal vehicles, influenced by IVECO being the cheaper end of the market, which was certainly noticed by drivers.

In 1999 Seddon Atkinson launched the Euromover for the refuse collection market. The OSCAR – One Step Cab Access – fitted to a normal chassis, yet gave a low mounting position forward of the engine. The step height of 380mm above ground level gave easy access both into and out of the vehicle and was intended to be considerably less tiring to crews operating these vehicles.

By July 2002 IVECO lost interest with Seddon Atkinson whilst concentrating on their own vehicles, believing the once leading British truck manufacturer had no future in Europe. So production at the Woodstock Factory ceased – saving a small fortune in business costs – and with little orders left on the books, they were transferred to Madrid, where Seddon Atkinson Vehicles became a name for imports only during its last grasp for sales. 150 staff were made redundant at Oldham, leaving only a handful to provide aftermarket support and sell trucks to UK customers. With odds stacked against them the small Seddon Atkinson team achieved an incredible 30% share of the refuse collection market.

In 2003, however, Seddon Atkinson's luck finally ran out, and inevitably announced its end of being a major supplier to the general haulage market. Instead they focused one last push on refuse and construction sectors, with rigid vehicles and the introduction of a 6x4 Tractor, an 8x4 two-spring suspension rigid and the Pacer, aimed towards their specialised customer base.

IVECO introduced a new cab for their EuroCargo range in 2005 whilst Seddon Atkinson engineers produced the necessary designs to adapt the cab for their 18 to 26-ton range of refuse collection and rigid vehicles. Seddon Atkinson's parent company IVECO decided to take the decision not to introduce Euro4 compliant engines into the Seddon Atkinson range, consequently – and suspiciously apparent – threw the plucky yet tired company to the wolves, ending production in October 2006.

I could go on explaining a little about other just as important British truck manufactures such as: AEC, Albion, Alexander Dennis, Argyle, Armstrong-Saurer, Austin, AWD, Baron, Bean, Beardmore, Bedford, Belsize Motors, Bristol, BMC (British Motor Corporation), Bruce-SN, Carmichael, Caledon, Commer, Crossley, Dennis Eagle, Dennis-Mann Egerton, Dodge (UK), Douglas, Ford (UK), Fowler, Garner, Garrett, Gilford, Guy, Halley, Hallford, Hardy, Haulamatic,

Jensen, Karrier, Kerr Stuart, Lacre, Lomount, Manchester, Mann, Maudslay, McCrud, Morris Commercial, Multiwheeler, Norde, Pagefield, Proctor, Quest, Rotinoff, Rowe-Hillmaster, Rutland, Sentinel, Shefflex, Star, Straker-Squire, Straussler, Thornycroft, Tilling Stevens, TVW, Union, Unipower, Vulcan, Yorkshire, and Zwicky. Apologies for missing any.

Sadly, all UK truck manufactures are long gone. And yet the manufactures I mention belong to an important history of truck innovators and designers, linked by a unique family. As for world-wide truck manufactures, there are too many to mention. Besides, who wants to know about those Johnny foreigner trucks?

Chapter 2

IMPORTANT BIG BITS

Fifth wheel coupling: The term 'fifth wheel' dates back to horse drawn carts with an axle fitted to the rear and a steering axle (turntable) at the front. The steering axle turned by means of a central fixed pin underneath the cart body that fits through a wheel fitted on top of the front axle – the 'fifth wheel' – acting like a bogie to allow the front wheels make a controlled turn.

Fast forward 600-years or so and the same principle of coupling a mechanism designed to fit onto articulate trucks was invented in 1911 by Charles H Martin, Wellville, Virginia, USA. But the first patented invention was improved by Charles E Bradshaw from Wellville, USA, in 1936, where a third of the patent was actually granted to Charles H Martin. However, it didn't take long for other engineers to improve the coupling.

Both world wars had a big influence on truck innovation, and by the Second World War the fifth wheel coupling mechanism kick-started manufacturing of semi-trailers and its ability to carry multiple, larger and heavier loads, accelerating the truck industry with new designs and technology. After which, we now have many semi-trailer variants including, box, skeletals, curtain siders, tippers, platforms, machine carriers, drawbar, refrigerant, tilt, recovery, low-loader, double-deckers... the list goes on.

Back in Frankfurt, Germany, Jost begun producing ball-bearing turntables in 1952. Four years later Jost started to produce fifth wheels for a fast growing articulated truck market we recognise today, complete with a lever-operated mechanism and a spring-loaded jaw release.

Trailers/semi-trailers: a trailer attached to a traction unit by a central kingpin that locates into the jaw of the coupling assembly mounted on the chassis of a prime mover. Semi trucks, also known as articulated lorries, at some point transport almost all goods we use across the world; either from ports, warehouses, distribution centres, factories, and alike. The use of articulated vehicles only became possible with the development of the semi-trailer, influencing a huge construction of major trunk roads articulated vehicles now thunder up and down to deliver your milk and bread today.

Car Transporters: Engineer, Alexander Winton, from Cleveland, Ohio, started to make cars in 1896. Two years later he sold his first car, and soon realised a need to speed up delivery to his customers spread far and wide, yet could only deliver one at a time. This also meant high delivery costs, wear and tear, even damage to the car before it had reached the customer. With these problems in mind Alexander solved his logistic headache by building a semi-truck to carry his cars. By 1899 the Winton Motor Carriage started to manufacture the world-first car transporter, quickly used by other car manufactures.

Alexander's first car transporter was nothing more than an adapted car that towed a cart. The platform of the cart sat on top of the car engine at the rear, resting on a pair of wheels at the front. A bit odd considering most cars and trucks had engines at the front. And the platform could only hold one car. However, the cart was mounted onto the pulling car, where the second purchased car was wheeled onto a ramp on the cart and lashed down onto the platform. The edge of the platform was then lifted off the ground and attached to the top of the rear of the pulling vehicle. Yes, a tad strange, but it worked.

By the 1930's American car salesman, George Cassens, further developed the innovation of transporting cars. He too was reliant on the relatively new specialist hauliers delivering cars to his dealership, so with a bit of thought and trade experience he developed the concept of delivering new cars direct from manufacturers straight to his customers, easing unnecessary transport costs. To make this new innovation cost effective he first needed a bigger trailer to carry more vehicles, so he devised a four-car carrier trailer pulled by a Dodge truck.

Another Engineer, John C. Endebrock, built horse-drawn carriages and used his skills to make, what he named, the Trailmobile: a chassis made of iron pulled by a Model T Ford car. It was user-friendly so anyone could hook it onto their Model T. However, the controls of a Model T is, let's say, different to modern cars. Nevertheless, John's trailer was so successful the concept of simplicity ensured the name Trailmobile is still used in the USA.

Fruehauf trailers: August Charles Fruehauf of Michigan, started his working life as a blacksmith and was asked to build a trailer to be towed behind, yet another, popular Model T Ford car. Mr. Frederic Sibley was so impressed with the trailer to haul his boat he asked August to build further trailers, termed semi-trailer. In 1918 August established the Fruehauf Trailer Company. Carter Manufacturing Company, manufacturing trailers since 1927 in Memphis, Tennessee, merged with August's company to become Fruehauf-Carter in 1947.

After 42-years of success Fruehauf-Carter developed financial difficulties and had to sell parts of the business to survive, resulting in re-naming the company as Fruehauf Trailer Corporation in 1989. But in 1996 the company fell into financial difficulties yet again and inevitably declared bankrupt. The axle plant in Ohio was sold to Holland Hitch Company, whilst the trailer sector went to Wabash National, USA.

King trailers: In Canada, Vern King started King Trailers in 1962 designing and manufacturing large platforms for heavy haulage and abnormal loads. The company spread its wings across the pond and grew to be the largest of its kind in the UK thanks to engineers producing bespoke trailers for many applications: transportation of aircraft fuselages, large plant, armoured military vehicles and even submarine sections.

In 1994 King Trailers developed additional units specialising in aerial access equipment. The new SkyKing brand, with partner, Palfinger Platforms, designed and manufactured a series of truck mounted access platforms, becoming market leader in the UK. By 2007 King Trailers became Transport Equipment Limited, designing and developing transport and handling solutions.

The skip: 'Who invented the skip?' once asked by Steve Coogan's hilarious character, Alan Partridge. But during the industrial revolution a 'skep' was nothing more than a basket on wheels where woven cotton was stored during its production process. The word skep was also used in the early industrial revolution years of the coal industry where coal was dug from a mine and measured as a skep when placed into a basket.

When rail tracks were introduced to mining a significant tonnage of coal could be transported from the pit face, but the old skeps – baskets – were simply not man enough to handle heavier loads. Larger and more industrial carriers were needed so wheeled steel and wood skeps were introduced to run on the tracks. Centuries later, as like many other English sayings, phrases and mispronunciations, the skep became known as a skip.

By the 1920s Edwin Walker, an employee at the Pagefield truck company in Southport, Lancashire, had the original idea of a sheet metal skip-like container mounted on a flatbed lorry to remove household general waste and transport in large bulk to landfill waste sites. The idea proved to be a success with Southport Borough Council, becoming known as the Pagefield system that used a 300-cubic Foot horse-drawn container.

Once the container was full of household refuse it was winched onto the back of a Pagefield flatbed truck and driven to a land-fill on the edge of town. But it wouldn't be for another forty-odd years before the skip we recognise today was made in Germany in the mid 1960's where it earned the term skip by way of its shape being similar to the old coal skep used in Victorian coal mines. Since, its shape has become synonymous with being placed on a driveway or side of a road full of rubble with an old mattress dumped on the top.

ISO Container: The principle use for a shipping container is to simply forward freight by combining shipping, railway and road haulage to distribute goods. ISO (International Shipping Organisation) shipping containers standardised construction and size to suit world-wide road transportation trailers. Also known as a cargo container, conex box, and when used for building construction or storage, a ISBU module (Intermodal Steel Building Unit).

American truck driver, Malcolm McLean, bought his first truck in 1934 during those early years when goods were boxed and packaged in all shapes and sizes. Loading or unloading of vehicles was painfully slow and cumbersome, often carried out by hand. He also noticed similar problems at the docks where freight unloaded from ships were either crated or gathered separately by ropes or cargo nets.

Malcolm expanded his business and became one of the largest haulage companies in the Southern States of America, later buying the Pan Atlantic Tanker Company, re-naming it Sea-Land Shipping. Remembering his observation of unloading ships, in 1956 he started to experiment with better efficient freight forwarding solutions by designing the first shipping container. It had to be durable for ocean travel, able to stack on top of one another whilst transported at sea, quick and easy to load, and suitable for road transportation.

US Navy, quick to notice the capabilities of Malcom's invention, recommended a standard size program – a military thing – and using a quick and simple twist-lock mechanism to clamp the container onto trailers and railroad freight wagons. By the 1970's Malcolm's original idea of a shipping container was truly recognised, with a little help from the US Navy, and now every shipping company around the world uses ISO containers to distribute goods. Progressively, goods from other countries became considerably cheaper to distribute and therefore cheaper to buy in shops, cutting freight forwarding costs by an unbelievable 90%.

The skeleton trailer naturally developed to carry a single 40ft or X2 20ft standard container. The shipping industry referred standard containers as a TEW for a 20ft and X TEW for the 40ft container for easy calculating quantities on ships. Less popular sizes include the supersized 53ft container, but the common variations remained as the 20ft and 40ft GP (General Purpose), 20ft and 40ft HQ (High Cube) which is 1ft higher than the standard GP version. There are also open top, open side, freezer & refrigerated, generator and welfare unit variants. They can be used for emergency or immediate housing by designing the internal space available into a 40ft static home, not unlike a holiday static home you would find on many seaside holiday resorts. They can also be stacked making them multi-story.

Diesel engine: Without the diesel engine there simply wouldn't be a truck industry we recognise today. Steam powered wagons were inefficient, uneconomical, heavy and unreliable in comparison to diesel powered trucks. Petrol engines offered less torque, too weak to pull heavy loads and incredibly thirsty. Its only niche in the automotive market became to power lighter vehicles such as cars, motorbikes, and vans.

Rudolf Diesel, born in Paris by German decent, started his working life as a refrigeration engineer, but his passion was engines. And because of his knowledge of heat transfer he designed a heat engine. He even designed and built a solar-powered air engine. In 1893 his heat engine, with a massive single 10ft iron cylinder and a huge heavy flywheel at its base, ran on its own generated heat. In 1894 he almost killed himself when his prototype exploded, but it didn't stop him filing for a patent.

Undeterred, he was adamant to make it work and prove his new engine could ignite a new cheaper fuel without using a spark. After two more years of tinkering and making further improvements he built another engine that demonstrated a theoretical efficiency of 75 % bearing in mind steam engines of that era struggled to reach 10 %. By 1898 Rudolf was so successful with his new engine it replaced many steam engine powered outlets including pump stations, generators, boats, and of course, trucks.

Gardner: Back in the UK engineers and inventors getting a whiff of the new engine didn't waste any time jumping on the latest technology band wagon. In 1868 Lawrence Gardner, a 28-year old machinist, went into business using a cellar that ran underneath four cottages in Upper Duke Street, Manchester. When tenants of the cottages defaulted on rent the landlord threatened to sell the workshop and all of Lawrence's equipment to pay towards arrears. Being a little desperate for cash he took out a loan with a building society and bought the cottages from his landlord to ensure security of his business premises in the cellar beneath.

Lawrence's business developed into making components for milling machines, tools, sewing machines, cutting equipment and steam engine parts. As the business grew his cellar workshop became too small to cope with demand, so he moved to larger premises in Cornbrook Park Road, Manchester, employing twelve staff.

In 1890 Lawrence died at only 50-years of age, leaving his wife, Anne, and sons, Thomas, Edward, Lawrence (Junior), Ernest and Joseph to run the business. Within a decade the family became a Limited Company, keeping the L. Gardner & Sons name in respect to Lawrence (Senior). The business, once again, relocated to Lund Street, Manchester, employing eighty staff.

L. Gardner & Sons Ltd., continued to manufacture machine products and even developed dynamos, one of which weighing an incredible 3-tons. They also developed a machine that cut rivets out of platinum wire for making false teeth and moulds for dentures.

In 1894 L. Gardner and Sons became the manufacturer of A. E. and H. Robinson's patented hot air engine, with a bore and stroke of 10-inches, developing less than 1hp. Heat was generated by burning coke in a firebox at a rate of 7 1/2 lb per hour creating 10% thermal efficiency, with no real difference to steam powered engines on the market. But its better reliability, economy, smaller size and weight created sales.

By 1899 L. Gardner & Sons were one of the first engineering manufactures to recognise growing interest in diesel technology, and diversified a little from hot air engines to concentrate on building their own design. The business outgrew premises once again and moved to Patricroft, Manchester, where in 1903 appointed Norris & Henty as sales agent to represent the company and its engines.

Three years later L. Gardner & Sons developed a 65hp paraffin engine. It had four vertical cylinders with an atmospheric burner for vaporising oil using a patented Simms-Bosch magneto. The centrifugal governor, operated by a direct timing gear from the lay-shaft, opened inlet valves and sparking assembly on a crude timing configuration. Inevitably a hit and miss principle. A lever from the governor adjusted flow of fuel into each cylinder and water injected into the engine to cool it when working a heavy load.

By 1914 the First World War took its inevitable effect on L. Gardner & Sons. Engine development accelerated whilst producing munitions and parts for heavy guns, as well as supplying gas engines for military vehicles, including the highly secretive development of the tank. After the war and into the 1920's Gardner continued rapid development with engine design, including the 4L2 marine engine and adapting it to fit into a bus. The engine became a success and quickly introduced the LW Series engine for trucks and other road vehicles.

During World War Two L. Gardner & Sons were commissioned by the Royal Navy to fit their LW Series into midget submarines. After the war LW Series production continued, finally superseded by the 150bhp LX Series fitted into trucks and buses. Gardner went on to produce the larger 6L3 and 8L3 Series engines fitted into locomotives and large boats.

The company became world export leaders of diesel engines for trucks, buses, marine and generator applications. And by 1950 through to the 1970's many British truck and bus manufacturers used the Gardner diesel engine range. However, the company became lethargic within its success, steadfast with tradition and refusing to design a turbocharged diesel engine. Predominately, they lost unit sales to other manufacturers overtaking them with turbocharged technology, offering economy, reliability and lower running costs.

Truck manufacturers realised engines with increased performance and better economy were the way forward. Engine manufacturers, such as Cummins Engine Company and Rolls Royce, were poised to pounce on the increasing market Gardner's couldn't or wouldn't exploit. The best Gardner engine available at the time was the 6LXC developing less than 200bhp. The new Cummins N Series, such as the non-turbo NH220 offered better power, fuel economy and reliability. With the introduction of the turbocharged NT Series and a power range from 240 to 320bhp allowed trucks to carry even heavier loads with more efficient fuel consumption.

L. Gardner & Sons had to catch up or go bust, so they hastily introduced a turbocharged version of the 10.5ltr 6LXC – the 6LXCT – producing only 230bhp. But it was too little too late; Gardner's success in the diesel engine industry was hit hard by fierce and superior competition. The Gardner 6LX Series remained in production until 1992 selling almost 100,000 units. But when euro1 emission restrictions were introduced the same year Gardner simply could not comply. The money to invest in new cleaner and leaner diesel engines wasn't available and inevitably L. Gardner & Sons ceased trading.

Perkins: Another Great British diesel engine pioneer was Frank Perkins from Peterborough, Cambridgeshire. Born in 1889 Frank developed light high-speed diesel engines whilst working for Aveling & Porter, Rochester. Until the 1930's diesel engines were large, extremely heavy and slow revving, offering less performance compared to petrol engines. But Frank believed diesel power was the future, and for smaller engines, convinced he could design a power unit comparable to the smaller size and performance of petrol engines.

Frank Perkins started his own company with Charles Chapman in 1932 working from a workshop in the centre of Peterborough, and set about developing their first engine – the Vixen. It started with the use of a cranking handle and heated combustion caps placed in four combustion chambers underneath the block, becoming the world's first high-speed diesel engine. By 1937 Perkins designed the P4 engine and soon afterwards the P6 developing 83bhp. A year later Perkins manufactured a series of engines called the Wolf, Lynx, Leopard I and II used in trucks, marine, agricultural and industrial applications.

F. Perkins Ltd., grew rapidly and soon needed larger premises, so Frank bought land in the Eastfield district of Peterborough to expand his company. The 1.6ltr P4C Series engine producing 45 to 60bhp became increasingly popular in Europe and Israel, fitted into taxis and small commercial vehicles such as Commer variants. In the late 1950's and early 1960's American taxis even had the P4C diesel engine fitted, with convertion kits made by Hunter NV of Belgium. Perkins engines were also factory-fitted to Jeep and Dodge light trucks.

By 1959 Perkins largest customer was the agricultural machinery giant, Massey Ferguson, and Frank sold the company to them but retained the Perkins engines name. The following year Perkins launched the six-cylinder 6.354 engine producing 112bhp. The unique design of this particular engine had a low camshaft with long pushrods to allow for a small timing case providing space for the water pump. Water cooling channels between cylinders and the bore itself were also designed smaller, making the engine compact enough to replace the larger V8 petrol engines.

Power output was increased to 120bhp and in 1962 a turbo charger was introduced, increasing power to 150bhp. American sales, however, remained low due to cheap petrol prices, and reliability was questioned compared to equivalent petrol engines. The 6.354 diesel engine was later re-developed to meet US and the EU controlled UK government's strict emissions standards, yet Perkins ceased production of this remarkable engine in 1996 after an incredible sales turnover of one million units.

In 1984 Perkins bought Rolls Royce Diesel International, renamed Perkins Engines (Shrewsbury) Ltd., to supply UK military engine requirements for the Foden EKA 6X6 and Scammell EKA 6X4 recovery vehicles, Leyland DROPS, and other large trucks and power generators. Ten years later Perkins bought Dorman Diesels, predominantly supplying power generators. Working together they produced the 4000 Series, based upon Dorman's design. Perkins also produced the 700 and 900 Series, supplying Caterpillar and NACCO the lift truck manufacturer, increasing unit sales to an amazing production total of 15 million units.

By purchasing Dorman Diesels, Perkins became a subsidiary of Lucas Varity. In 1998 Perkins was bought by another industrial vehicle giant and former customer, Caterpillar Inc., becoming, arguably – by Cummins mainly – the world's largest heavy diesel engine manufacturer, worth a staggering $1.3 billion. Perkins now developed engines in the UK, USA, Brazil, India, Japan and China for hundreds of applications.

Perkins continued to build a new series of quieter, more powerful and fuel-efficient engines that had to conform to ever tighter US and EU controlled emissions standards. These new-age diesel engines are still used in the 21st Century in construction, industrial, marine, material-handling and power-generation applications, including a range of gas engines. A new facility in Georgia, USA, was built in 2003 to produce the 400 Series engine for American and Brazilian customers. Back in Blighty, however, world markets tend to shift like the tide and Perkins was forced to reduce production in 2012.

Cummins: In the USA early diesel engine technology received a poor reception, mainly due to its unreliability and performance compared to its petrol counterpart. But Clessie L Cummins of Columbus, Ohio, a self-taught mechanic, was confident to prove the diesel engine could be a reliable and economical source of power. In 1919 he started his own company, the Cummins Engine Company, with William Glanton Irwin, a local banker, who was already an investor in Clessie and his machine shop repairing agricultural machinery. Soon after building his own designs Clessie found his first customer, Sears Roebuck & Co. Unfortunately the engines proved to be unreliable and defective.

Almost a decade later, and an increasingly nervous investor, Clessie fitted one of his improved engines into a Packard limousine and took Irwin for a spin in America's first diesel-powered car. Irwin was impressed, to the point of investing even more nervous cash into the fledgling engine company, helping to finance further tests of the car and entering it in the Indianapolis Motor Speedway in 1931. Along with Irwin, the event raised huge interest in Clessie's new engine design.

In 1933 Clessie produced the H Series, which became a huge success within the American trucking industry. In 1934 J. Irwin Miller, great-nephew of W.G. Irwin, became general manager, eventually leading Cummins Engine Company to international recognition. Amazingly, considering Cummins success, didn't earn a profit until 1937, but was totally assured by his own ingenuity offering a 100,000-mile warranty on all of his engines.

After the Second World War USA government invested in a huge Trans-American Highway construction project and Cummins engines powered many of the plant equipment that built it. With the newly constructed highway haulage companies wanted reliable engines to power their trucks along the thousands of miles of freshly laid tarmac, demanding durability, power and economy.

Cummins Engine Company assured with confidence that the American truck industry can rely upon Cummins diesel engines to deliver what they wanted. The American truck manufacturers, persuaded by testimonial advertising of Cummins reliability, power and economy, begun to believe in the product and by the late 1950's unit sales exceeded $100 million.

Cummins Engine Company, thanks to the Trans-American Highway construction project, continued to grow and felt confident to start its international recognition. In

1956 Cummins built an engine production facility in Shotts, Scotland, and through the 1960's J. Irwin Miller forged strong ties with Europe, China, India, Mexico, Brazil and Japan, eventually expanding an impressive sales network to around 2,500 dealers in 98 countries.

By the 1970's Cummins introduced the K Series, predominately produced for large plant vehicles, locomotives and generator sets. Not forgetting the enormous K series V16 3,067bhp engine powering many applications including oil and gas rigs in the North Sea. The introduction of the N Series became a breakthrough in diesel engine technology, and with the introduction of turbochargers to the NT Series, created the demise of L. Gardner & Sons.

The tried and tested V Series, such as the V903 mainly used in the marine industry, V504 and VT555 in plant vehicles, begun to phase out in the early 1980's, along with the N Series. The replacement was a revolutionary lighter L Series, introduced with a single 6-cylinder head, rather than individual twin heads for the 6-cylinder N series. The L10, a 10-litre turbocharged engine producing 250 to 320bhp, increased power output over the years by further development in fuel pump and mapping technology.

The L10 finally reached its pinnacle with the introduction of the 6-cylinder 11-litre M11 Series, with a power range output exceeding 500bhp. This enormous power output from an inline 6cyl engine became the envy of many rival manufacturers producing higher fuel consumption V8 engines with similar power. It was also lighter than the L10 with even better overall economy.

Introduction of the smaller B and C Series turbo-charged 6cyl engines were developed for smaller applications, recognising that Perkins had a huge percentage of the small diesel engine market. So the introduction of the B and C Series engines were designed to narrow the market share, fitting the new engine into applications such as buses, smaller HGV's, even UK armoured military vehicles. For applications any smaller the engines were simply too big to compete with Perkins within the smaller material-handling equipment – small forklift trucks and road vehicles under 7.5-tonnes.

Although Cummins Engine Company failed to enter the smaller engine market – most probably because it simply didn't need to – the N and L series had a brilliant trick up its sleeve, being, yet again, the envy of rival manufactures, especially during the era of poor quality diesel fuel waxing in extreme cold temperatures.

In the bad old days – pre 1990's – diesel was a very poor quality fuel. After all, it's a by-product of petrol – the lower end of oil refinery. Additives are mixed with other chemicals into the diesel to preserve its octane level and prevent it from degrading. But waxing – a chemical residue created by cold temperatures – remained a problem due to the lack of a suitable chemical available that would prevent waxing without compromising the efficiency of the fuel. The only alternative was to heat up diesel in the fuel tank before it entered the engine – thus prevent engine failure.

Cummins engines, however, thanks to a unique injection system, didn't need expensive fuel tank warmers due to the entire engine acting like a fuel pump, initially pumping fuel around the engine before it reached the injectors. This was done by the fuel distributor, commonly mistaken as a fuel pump, and the only immediate warming came from a fuel heater – looking not unlike a filter – powered by the first ignition stage. Once turned on, any remaining cold fuel in pipes will receive enough heat before entering the injection system, thus starting in extreme cold weather conditions.

In 1986 Cummins Engine Company bought the Onan Corporation from Cooper Industries that originally manufactured automotive test equipment and tooling. In later years they designed and built generators first produced in 1926 and by the 1940's became the largest supplier of generators for the US military. Today Cummins – arguably – is the world's largest producer of large diesel engines – around 50% total global ownership. They also distribute Holset turbochargers and engine filtration – Fleetguard & Nelson filters.

Other than diesel engine production Cummins has a further three interests: Power Generation, Components Business, and Distribution, supplied to around 150 countries, having a turnover of a staggering $17 billion in 2013. The company employ almost 46,000 staff in 197 countries around the world. A truly influential global company.

Chapter 3

JUST AS IMPORTANT SMALLER BITS

When Wilhelm Maybach designed and built the first truck powered by an internal combustion engine the braking system was nothing more than an adaptation of a primitive invention used by the Romans – a wooden lever that depressed a simple wooden block against a wooden wheel to slow the cart down by use of friction.

Maybach and Daimler, including many coach and cart builders before them, faced a recurring problem with the wooden block friction brake – brake fade. Yes, even early pioneers suffered from it. This was solved – sort of – by wrapping a piece of leather around the wooden block to give a better and almost constant friction during braking to a full stop whilst preventing block and wheel wear. But it wasn't Daimler or even Maybach who invented the first brake shoe.

When Karl Benz built his first car, his wife Bertha and two teenage sons, Richard and Eugen, took it for a spin unbeknown to Karl. One early August morning in 1888 she decided to drive Karl's invention from Mannheim to Pforzheim, Germany, to visit her parents. During the bone-shaking drive Bertha noticed when using the brake it started to smoulder caused by friction when slowing down the vehicle, and feared the wheel may actually catch fire let alone fail to stop the car.

Bertha carried out the world first pit-stop at a Blacksmith workshop and asked for help to cool down the brake. The Blacksmith obliged by pouring water onto the hot brake lever, and it was at that moment Bertha had a brain-wave: wrap a piece of wet leather around the block of wood, inadvertently inventing the brake shoe.

The Blacksmith found a piece of old leather, tied it around the brake block, and bingo – a lined brake shoe, albeit a Heath Robinson affair. Bertha continued her 120-mile journey after making another world first – a fuel stop – at a pharmacy in Wiesloch, to refuel with 10-litres of ligroin (petrol hadn't been invented yet).

Unbelievably early locomotives also used a wooden block against a wheel. Thankfully, and considering the size and weight of trains, improvements in materials such as cast iron brake shoes were quickly adapted. But even this innovation eventually proved to be inadequate, and a much stronger and reliable method was needed to stop heavy trains let alone trucks – the air braking system, originally created for locomotives but improved and adapted to fit onto heavy road vehicles.

WABCO: Locomotive air brake system was invented in 1869 by George Westinghouse, New York, USA, where his company Westinghouse Air Brake Company (WABCO) established into one of the most successful air brake companies in the world.

George's unique and revolutionary system was based upon a triple valve configuration supplied by compressed air that inverted the action of the direct air brake. Air supplied by rubber hoses from a reservoir tank fitted beneath the carriage charged the system and released the brakes via a spring brake chamber, where air pressure through a valve kept the brakes open. Draining air applied the brakes via a footbrake valve to release air from the system. The configuration was responsive and close to being fail-safe, becoming a pre-requisite in air brake systems today.

Knorr-Bremse: In 1905 George Knorr also manufactured brakes for locomotives and railway wagons, and by 1922 the company diversified into the commercial vehicle industry. Knorr-Bremse was the first European Company to develop a pneumatic system that applied all vehicle and trailer brakes simultaneously, and by 1925 most larger trucks had all-wheel air brakes. In 1949 air brake systems became standard on most heavy trucks, semi-trailors, draw-bars and buses. By the 1960's air brake technology for HGV's developed automatic slack adjusters, air dryers, dual brake valves and first generation antilock braking systems (ABS).

EBS: In the 1950s electronic braking system technology was already fitted to motorbikes, then introduced to luxury cars a decade later. But it wasn't until 1978 when Bosch and Daimler-Benz Company developed the first fully electronic multi-channel ABS for trucks. Since the addition of computer-controlled brake sensors led to the effectiveness of ABS, innovative leaps of technology eventually headed towards a complete EBS (Electronic Braking System).

WABCO pioneered the EBS in 1996 first fitting the system to a Mercedes-Benz Actros. Then in 1998 the TEBS (Trailer Electronic Braking System) for trailers quickly followed suit. The electronic signal created for actuating EBS brakes is still energised by compressed air but the air pressure is fully controlled by the electronic control unit (ECU) to deliver a more responsive, accurate and stable braking.

The modulation characteristics via Electronic Control Unit (ECU) programming can be tailored to suit different vehicle manufacturer requirements, where ideally the trailer will also have TEBS fitted so the prime mover (tractor unit) EBS that has the capability to electronically talk to the TEBS via the ECU and initiate braking in almost perfect synchronisation.

Exhaust brake: Brake fade is caused when friction absorbs energy from movement to the point of failing against a force when applied for a prolonged duration. So an additional braking system is required to assist the main air brakes to slow a heavy vehicle down without the use of applying friction brakes. A retarder – exhaust brake – is an auxiliary device that provides a braking force using spent energy from the engine. The energy absorbing capability of retarders are mainly used to assist with travelling down a steep hill and driving in adverse conditions including ice and snow.

Common types of retarders are engine brakes, exhaust brakes, electromagnetic, and hydrodynamic applications. Engine brakes absorb energy by converting a diesel engine into an air compressor and hydraulically opens the exhaust valves at the end of the compression stroke. This particular braking system is fitted to diesel engines that power a manual transmission creating drag with each selected gear. However, such a system isn't suitable for vehicles fitted with automatic transmissions due to pressure required for each gear selection.

A more favourable retarder application is fitted after the exhaust manifold creating back pressure on the engine exhaust by closing a valve. This particular retarder isn't effective at low speeds, but it is a cheaper option. The retarder still provides reasonable performance in long downhill braking, though, when configured with the correct unit and trailer.

Electromagnetic retarders create a restricting force by shearing magnetic flux lines. These retarders are mainly used on heavy-duty HGV's and even buses. But they are clumbersum, extremely heavy and have a complicated installation process. Once fitted they work quite effectively but create a huge power drain on the electrical system.

Hydrodynamic retarders are brakes that produce retardation by shearing oil. The kinetic energy created by shearing is converted into heat, then dissipated indirectly to the engine cooling system producing drag whilst the engine retains enough oil to lubricate itself. Hydrodynamic retarders are used in some bus and heavy duty vehicle applications, but the system effects fuel economy.

Exhaust emission regulations: By the mid 1970's the European Economic Countries (EEC) – the Common Market (later re-invented as the EU) – implemented agencies to restrict exhaust emissions throughout all European Member States. Vehicle manufactures replied with the PCV (Positive Crankcase Ventilation) system, drawing crankcase fumes, heavy in unburned hydrocarbons, into the engine intake. The unburned hydrocarbons are then ignited for a second time rather than released from the crankcase into atmosphere.

The first legislated exhaust emission standards were enforced by the State of California in 1966. By 1968 the rest of the USA quickly followed suit. Further tougher emission standards introduced in 1975 highlighted the need of catalytic converters to all cars for implementing after-treatment of exhaust gasses. But it wasn't possible with existing leaded fuel due to the residue of lead contaminating the platinum catalyst.

The production and distribution of unleaded fuel was a major challenge, not to mention the sudden transition for manufacturers to be compliant by law, including European Common Market member States. All modern cars are now equipped with catalytic converters and leaded fuel is almost impossible to purchase in most countries.

The EEC control over regulation of emissions created further member government agencies to enforce their own laws. The EEC and all its members voted on policies setting limits where each Member State decided how best to enforce them in their own country. In the UK regulations concerning environmental policies are known as devolved powers and controlled by the government, to an extent.

Engine efficiency steadily improved with the introduction of electronic ignition, fuel injection metering and computerised engine management. Advances in engine and vehicle technology continued to reduce exhaust gasses but created further engine expense through servicing and replacing expensive exhaust systems. And even with 21st Century technology low emission targets set by naïve governments remains insufficient and impossible to meet.

DPF: Incomplete combustion of diesel fuel produces carbon particles commonly known as soot. These particles include tiny nano-particles smaller than a thousandth of a millimetre – one micron. Hastily rushed through a manufacturing process to please EU governments, thus pacifying emission regulations, diesel particulate filters (DPF) remove up to 90% of soot before expelled to atmosphere. In certain conditions a DPF can remove 99.9% or 0.001 gram of soot particles per one kilometre, but at a price.

Some filters are single-use, which is an expensive option, intended for disposal and replacement once full of accumulated soot. For an HGV this is around an average of 240,000 to 380,000 miles, depending on application – stop/start deliveries, long haul, construction... and so on. An alternative system is designed to burn off the accumulated particulate either naturally through the use of a catalyst or by active means such as a fuel burner that heats the filter to high combustion temperatures.

This is accomplished by engine programming to run when the filter is full or produces high amounts of NOX (Nitrogen Oxide) to oxidise the accumulated soot, or through other methods by revving the engine at high speed for around twenty-minutes, known as regeneration. However, it isn't always successful and may require a complete DPF replacement, which is also expensive to replace.

Cleaning is required as part of periodic maintenance, and it must be done carefully to avoid damaging the filter. Failure to do so can easily create damage from oil contamination caused by the fuel injectors and turbochargers, resulting in further component damage to the engine. Vehicles driven exclusively at low speeds in urban traffic require periodic trips at higher speeds to clean the DPF. The regeneration process occurs at road speeds higher than those generally applied on city streets.

Particulate filters have been fitted to industrial diesel engines since 1980 and vehicle variants since 1985. But diesel engine emissions were not regulated until 1987 in the USA and later, surprisingly, in Europe. It wasn't until anticipation of the future Euro 5 regulations in 2000 Peugeot Citroën became the first manufacture to fit DPF assemblies as standard on to their cars. By 2012 DPF systems were first fitted to HGV's to meet the new Euro 6 exhaust emissions regulations coming into force.

The downside for manufactures of HGV's having to fit DPF systems, and inevitably the end user – the customer – is a huge cost. Truck DPF assemblies are usually enveloped within the exhaust silencer, also know as a chemical factory, open to all weathers and damage, costing around £7,000 to replace. The precious metals within the DPF are also a sort-after favourite by thieves, where many vehicles have been targeted over the years. Even small vans fall foul, where the vehicle is jacked up to get at the DPF from underneath.

Mud flap: Not as insignificant as you may think. The humble mud flap comes in many sizes, using ribbed, smooth or even suppressor atomising designs. Manufactuters have improved on the original, including associated parts such as brackets, hangers and mountings. But the first mud flap goes to Oscar Glenn March, an inventor who, mistakenly, failed to patent his invention. Obviously someone else quickly exploited this by improving his invention and patented it, thus, officially, inventing the mud flap. But for the sake of originality we'll stick with Oscar.

Oscar fought in the Second World War, serving in both the army and Airforce. After the war he worked as a driver for 40-years, retiring in 1983. Upon his retirement he won awards such as the Meritorious Civilian Service Award, the second highest civilian award given by the U.S. government; the Oklahoma Meritorious Service Medal; Oklahoma City's Ambassador-at-Large award; and the Distinguished Alumni award from Langston University where he attended for two-years prior to the war. In total he received a staggering 87 awards for achievements and commendation.

It was when he was working as a driver at the Tinker airbase he noticed large trucks kicking up rocks, grit, mud and debris-filled surface water, damaging expensive airfield radar equipment positioned around the base. Delicate cargo and even passing personnel were struck as trucks rumbled by. So he came up with the idea of attaching sections of tarpaulin onto straps and securing them onto the chassis next to the rear of the tyre.

After a few improvements his design was attached to every truck on the base preventing further damage to radar equipment and personnel. His canvas design is still being used by the airbase today. And because of the safety aspect of his invention it is now law to fit mud flaps to all road trucks.

Turbo charger: Amazingly the first close proximity of a pump to boost power output out of an engine was invented by Gottlieb Daimler in 1885 when he was developing his first car. He patented his design of a gear driven pump that forced air injection into the engine intake. Technically he invented the supercharger rather than the turbo, but forced injection was invented nonetheless. Even Rudolf Diesel in 1896 had a bash at developing an injection pump that forced air into the combustion chamber to increase fuel efficiency and power output.

It wasn't until 1905 did the actual turbocharger we recognise today become reality, invented and patented by Swiss engineer, Alfred Buchi. But his first prototype wasn't fitted to an engine until the outbreak of the First World War, where it was used on an aircraft radial engine. Between the First and Second World Wars his turbochargers were tried on diesel generator and marine engines, and by the 1950's trucks had turbochargers to diesel engines. It took a further two decades before car manufacturers dared to fit a turbo on their production line petrol and diesel applications.

Scania and Volvo also started to use turbochargers in the 1950's but found them to be too large, clumbersum and unreliable for their engine applications, supplied by turbo manufacturer Elliot & Eberspacher. It wasn't until 1954 Volvo could confidently produce their own first turbo diesel powered truck, the TD96AS, increasing the power output by 35bhp to 185bhp.

In the same year Cummins Engines recognised the importance of the turbocharger and developed the 6-cylinder JT, NT and NRT range, and the huge 12 cylinder VT12 diesel engine. Holset became the turbo industry leader and was soon bought by Cummins Engines, where Cummins now had the most reliable turbochargers fitted to the most reliable diesel engines in the world.

By 1990 the first European heavy-duty wastegate turbocharger was put into production by Scania and Holset technology that improved power and fuel economy. And with Holset knowledge and experience in 1998 they developed the first variable geometry turbo, but the teething problems persisted with this type of turbo technology and turbo shafts tended to break, causing huge repair bills for the truck owners.

To remedy some turbo issues additional oil changes were introduced to service intervals, which did help. More drastic maintenance was to change the turbo at a given mileage before it failed – bit of guesswork – so to prevent failure on the road, recovery bills and productive downtime.

The Pallet: The pallet as we know it today comes in all shapes and sizes depending upon the load. But it has to have started from somewhere. And that can be a little tricky, because believe it or not, there is an argument over the invention of this simple yet effective addition to the haulage industry. So let's start with Howard Hallowell.

According to Howard, back in 1923 he didn't name his invention a pallet. It was called a lift truck platform. And the reason he invented this platform was due to the recently invented forklift truck kept damaging goods when moving them around the docks, yards and warehouses. So making a platform for goods to be secured on avoided damage from the forklifts and other hazards.

The other claimant to have invented the pallet is George Raymond, along with William House, in 1930, and they called their invention a sled. But their sled had a few differences to previous pallets: made out of cheaper wood without using metal feet, and a bottom deck with a gap spacing for forklift tines allowing easier access and stacking.

With the outbreak of World War Two, pallets were utilised to transport millions of tonnes of weapons, ammunition, vehicle and aircraft parts, armour, clothing, food and many other supplies needed to keep the war machine moving. And when the war ended pallets continued to serve the nation, as well as the Empire moving goods around the globe.

In 1954 a standard pallet size 48X40 inches was conceived so to amalgamate a conversion between rail and truck transportation. And today [2021] 250,000,000 pallets transport goods around the UK. And the UK manufactures around 55,000,000 pallets per year, producing and using more than any other EU country.

Chapter 4

EVOLUTION OF THE VOCATIONAL DRIVER

It's all very well mentioning pioneers and inventors of automotive development, but a truck is useless without a driver to operate it. Strictly speaking Wilhelm Maybach drove the first truck and so the obvious choice for recruiting pioneer drivers were those that designed and built them, but you can only drive one truck at a time.

So drivers from tried and tested steam powered wagons, although apprehensive of the new contraption, nervously took that huge leap into the unknown murky territory of the internal combustion engine. The new automotive technology even attracted a curious attention from locomotive engineers, previously steadfast in a belief that steam power could never be superseded.

Training, however, was non-existent, having only a little verbal and practical instruction from the designer and fledgling mechanics that maintained them. After which trial and error became the curriculum. It wasn't until the invention of pneumatic tires, enclosed cabs, smooth running engines and easier to use gearboxes did drivers appreciated a more reliable truck to travel at much higher speeds over cobbled roads originally made for the much slower horse and cart. And in 1912 the introduction of the electric headlight allowed the driver to travel at night in relative safety.

As more and more operators of early trucks became confident with the new and fast moving technology, it wasn't long before those with an entrepreneurial flare realised the potential of haulage and the increasing need it demanded. Companies using the new technology included SW Wrefords of Northampton, founded in 1904 by Silvanus William Wreford, were amongst the first, and still going strong in the 21st Century [2021].

Just as quick to emerge were the specialist hauliers using vehicles designed by manufactures such as G. Scammell & Nephew. Drivers of these particular heavy trucks, however, were few and far between. So the heavy haulage industry didn't really establish a niche market until post World War One, where soldiers that predominately served with the Army Service Corps gained experience driving large vehicles. Service Corps drivers became experts at towing heavy guns with a team of six horses, driving staff cars, ambulances, trucks and even tanks.

At first they retained their rank of private, but once trained became distinguishable from infantry soldiers by wearing a similar uniform to the Light Horse Regiment. Subtle differences were their peaked cap and leather putties rather than the canvas type. They were also amongst the first to create courses for various vehicle types and develop vehicle competency training for horse-drawn wagons, steam and petrol powered vehicles.

Being a driver rather than an infantry soldier certainly wasn't an easy alternative to being bogged down in the trenches and putting up with wizz-bangs, mortars and machine gun fire. Drivers were essential for bringing much needed food, ammunition, weapons and equipment to the front line, and transported wounded to field hospitals under fire more often than not. Targeted by enemy snipers, machine gunners and even artillery, it was a dangerous job and their courage soon gained respect from other corps and regiments throughout the British army.

Once the war ended Great Britain went through many changes, one of which was the haulage industry. Factories that once produced munitions and fighting equipment for the war effort returned to civilian production. Many companies jumped at the opportunity to exploit further potential business due to a high demand for heavy industry parts and components. That meant a need for more trucks to deliver them, in particular larger trucks with the ability to tow trailers and deliver heavier loads. Of course there were now fully experienced and skilled drivers to operate them.

The sudden influx of road haulage companies after the war complemented further entrepreneurs to start a delivery business – the original white van man. Traditional delivery of goods from factory to train station using steam-powered traction engines and even horse-drawn wagons along pot-holed dirt tracks and cobbled streets was still a common place. But powerful railway companies begun to realise the petrol-powered trucks had developed into a long-haul vehicle – a road train – threatening business and profit.

By the 1920's and even during the great depression, road links between towns and cities started to improve with the introduction of the numbering system for A-roads, concentrating upon a pattern to reflect its importance, the A1 being the first: London to Edinburgh (397 miles). Along with truck technology manufactures and other businesses realised road hauliers could now deliver direct to customers rather than waste time and money on multiple transhipment between local wagons (steam powered or horse drawn) onto railway carriages, then onto other local wagons.

Forward thinking haulage companies quick to cash in on this new delivery concept invested in larger fleets, employed more drivers and offered even further long-distance services. As trucks travelled further, fuel stations were few and far between. More often than not it was the local pharmacy that sold gasoline, but not the quantities needed for a thirsty lorry.

The only way to ensure heavy commercial vehicles could reach their destination and return back to base was to carry enough fuel with them. That meant fitting huge fuel tanks and the ability to carry spare fuel in cans. Drivers also had to be mechanically minded to carry out breakdown repairs and maintenance en-route. Even take spare parts should there be a need to replace failed components. And because sleeper cabs and cab heaters were yet to be invented, it was a good idea to take a tent, warm blankets, fresh change of clothes and a camping stove, as days away from home were becoming common place.

By the 1930's driving a truck became a vocation rather than an added duty to a job description. Yet drivers still didn't require any compulsory training other than to rely upon trained and experienced drivers from the army and civilians that had learnt the hard way involving many, many mishaps and accidents. After the truly mechanised Second World War trucks were abundant, and many drivers with the required skills gained from the likes of Royal Army Service Corps (RASC), Royal Tank Regiment(s) (RTR), Royal Artillery (RA),

Royal Engineers (RE) and the Royal, Electrical & Mechanical Engineers (REME) were ready available.

Great Britain took a huge beating to defeat Nazi Germany, rewarded with becoming almost skint – yet again – for saving the world from global tyranny. The government at the time drew plans to get the country back on its feet; quickly realising the best place to start was a massive investment in its road network. A-roads were repaired, resurfaced and new roads, including dual carriageways, were constructed to either link or coincide with old routes. More refuelling stations were constructed selling diesel as well as petrol, and the first purpose-built transport cafés catered for trucks started to appear, allowing weary drivers to park overnight within the café grounds.

Arrival of the 1950's brought an ever increasing number of HGV's thundering up and down the highways and byways carrying heavier loads at much faster speeds. So the much-needed motorway was developed allowing traffic to travel at high speed with no interruption or restriction. And the first stretch of motorway in the UK was opened on 5th December 1958 near Preston, Lancashire: an eight-mile by-pass around the city called the M6.

With a combination of improved trunk roads lacing the country and more powerful trucks the driver became more and more under pressure to deliver goods on time. It wasn't uncommon to drive constantly for twenty hours without a break just to get a cargo to its destination and thus paid for the delivery.

The advent of a universal fifth wheel in the 1950's and the much improved diesel engine to pull heavier loads meant the tractor unit could uncouple a trailer to load at source, leaving the tractor unit to collect a loaded one. The articulated lorry had come of age, with the ability to pull trailers from various suppliers loaded with goods direct to customers or make a pre-arranged meet with another truck so to swap trailers.

This meant goods could be taken up and down the country without the need to pick up from warehouses or factories en-route to further the destination. The outcome, however, also created long driving hours to keep up with demand. And without any commercial driver regulations or restrictions, no need for a HGV driving licence and very little training, the result was inevitable – accidents.

Although truck technology had evolved leaps and bounds since Wilhelm Maybach crude invention, driver comfort dragged its heels in development, albeit having a basic solid wooden seat. As for protection, this was nothing more than the distance between a driver's face and the windscreen separated by a huge solid steel steering wheel. Cabs were also extremely drafty, letting cold wind and rain in between ill-fitting doors and windscreen seals, side windows and the cab floor. Oh, of course, there were also no seatbelts. Cab heaters weren't introduced to commercial vehicles until the late 1950's and they were poor in performance. Nothing like the sophisticated heating systems we enjoy today.

Harsh winters coursed problems with not only starting a diesel engine – waxing of fuel and poor battery crank-turning power – the de-icing of windscreens came down to simply removing ice with a scraper. But keeping the windscreen from icing or misting during travel was a pain. Drivers had to either keep stopping to scrape off ice inside and outside of the windscreen. This particular practise carried on until the

1970's when truck manufacturers realised the importance of de-icing and more efficient heaters.

Off course, during the summer months drivers of trucks had to endure the heat as well as ill-insulated cabs, where air-conditioning was only seen in expensive cars such as Rolls Royce and Jaguar. Haulage companies, and therefore truck manufacturers, had a selfish belief that an expensive luxury, such as heating and air conditioning, was far too expensive for a common working man to enjoy. After all, they were employed labour to drive trucks, not limousines.

Seatbelts started to appear in cars during the 1960s – Volvo being the first – and took a further decade to see them regularly fitted in HGV's. But just like the car not many drivers wore them. Excuses such as discomfort or even never worn as didn't see the point, past many lips of car and truck drivers alike. Others were of the opinion that seatbelts were restrictive and would trap them in the event of an accident, if the vehicle caught fire or that if a seatbelt wasn't being used and the driver was thrown forward and knocked out, then they'd burn to death anyway.

Statistics have shown that 1/10 HGV drivers suffered further injuries due to wearing a seatbelt after an accident. Of course, the injuries could have been a lot worse if not worn. I for one have seen too many battered cabs with splashes of claret covering the drivers side due to not wearing a seatbelt. So I think I'll hedge my bets with odds of 1/10 and join the other 9 by wearing mine.

EU Health & Safety regulations state that a radio must be fitted into HGV's to give disassociated background noise by helping to prevent feeling drowsy due to the monotonous drone of an engine, vehicle motion and constant road surface noise. Before the requirement of radios they were seen as a luxury and weren't fitted as standard until the mid- 1970's in Volvo trucks. With the invention of portable transistor radios, however, many drivers took their own radios to entertain them upon a long journey.

The problem with portable radios were the cabs of the late 1960's to early 1980's had poor installation against road and engine noise, so drivers tended to place a thick blanket over the ill-fitting engine cover to dampen down noise and drafts. But small transistor radios, even at full volume, were still difficult to hear. Reception was also a problem – the FM radio signal was yet to be invented, so Medium or Long Wave were the only options. And when driving under a bridge or tunnel, or passing a tall building, street lamps or electricity pylons, the signal became distorted, crackled or even lost, let alone the momentous whistling caused by atmospherics or interference from the engine electronics.

The signal was also weak due to the bare metal cab and the radio synchronised itself with the engine as the signal distortion raised and lowered with the speed of the engine revs. Even today [2021] try listening to 'TalkSport' or Radio5 Live on AM you'll see what I mean. Thankfully radio cassette players became popular by the 1980's but even these had problems with chewing tapes. You still, however, had the old faithful, should you wish to be entertained whilst driving up and down the nations highways and byways – CB (Citizen Band) radio.

Early CB radios were imported from America in the 1970's and used different frequency bands. Their popularity exploded thanks to films such as 'Convoy' and 'Smokey and the Bandit,' quickly becoming the perfect communication device amongst truck drivers. Although legal to own but strangely illegal to use in the UK they weren't legalised for use until 2nd November 1981 providing they were adapted to use the legal 27 Mhz airwave frequency, and of course pay a £15 licence fee at the post office for the privilege.

Enthusiasts and clubs started to crop up around the country but the CB craze started its demise due to channels becoming too crowded. Some CB operators abused the airwaves by continuously pressing their microphone button to play music. And although burners were used to boost a signal, these devices wiped out any signal for normal operators within a given range to broadcast. The use of foul language constantly used by others also contributed to its demise and many users simply lost interest.

After only a few years of popularity the CB radio finally died a quiet death thanks to the technological breakthrough of personal communication devices – the in-cab telephone. Of course, driving whilst talking on a mobile device is very naughty and now illegal, but back in the 1980's the dangers were yet to be discovered on how easy it is to be distracted, especially when driving through towns, cities, motorways... you know the rest.

Talking of towns and cities, former Mayor of London, conservative MP (Member of Parliament) and now Prime Minister [2021] Boris Johnson will have you believe London is no different to any other part of the UK. HGV drivers, however, disagree. Even as far back as the 1760's traffic has always been extremely congested with little or no driving discipline. Yet professional HGV drivers have always been accused, blamed, renounced and hated since the first trucks appeared on city roads.

When articulated vehicles became popular, council planners of large towns and cities, in particular London, were slow, or even stagnant on the uptake to accommodate HGV's upon its roads. Many towns and cities, especially London, still have warehouses and factories with ancient back streets originally designed for horse and carts to access them. Many yards are still only accessible by reversing, and using an articulated vehicle to negotiate the manoeuvre isn't easy through a blind-sided narrow gateway.

Tight T-junctions are a problem for HGV's, in particular for articulated vehicles when there are further obstacles in the middle of the road, such as traffic light islands or crossing barriers, having little choice but take up both lanes to turn left. At the same time idiotic car drivers that are supposed to recognise an HGV's requirement to use all of the road – check your Highway Code – accuse truck drivers as being arrogant. But not that long ago driving a licensed truck, including negotiating difficult junctions, wasn't a legal requirement.

Until 1970 HGV drivers didn't need a vocational licence, let alone a separate category. All that was required was a normal car licence without limited capacity of 3-tons between the ages of 17 and 21. Above the age of 21 a car licence automatically allowed a driver to drive most type of trucks, including articulated vehicles. Later in the same year the government introduced a new classification of vehicle – Goods Vehicle – where training and a test was finally required to pass before driving them.

A panic ensued amongst truckers with the thought of having to take another driving test, but established and experienced drivers didn't need to worry as they had acquired (grandfather) rights that allowed them to drive

HGV's without the need for a further test. For those that wished to pursue an HGV career after 1970 a new test beckoned. The new HGV licence, however, was automatically issued to those that had been driving HGV's for a full period during the six months previous. But 'Acquired Rights' drivers had to be proven by their employers to the Ministry of Transport – now known as the Driver and Vehicle Standards Agency (DVSA) [formally known as the Driver and Vehicle Licensing Agency (DVLA)].

The new licence was first categorised into eight classes, depending on the size and commercial use of the vehicle. Drivers that had operated articulated trucks with manual gearboxes (which were most) for the previous six months before the introduction of the new licence were issued with an HGV 'All Classes' licence. Drivers that had driven smaller rigid trucks, such as a 5-ton 4-wheeler, were restricted to that particular vehicle size and class.

To drive anything larger needed the requirement of a further test to have the 'All Classes' category on their licence. PSV (Passenger Service Vehicle) driving tests, however, didn't become compulsory until May 1985. Up until then, it was the Traffic Commissioner that decided whether or not local applicants took the test.

Working long hours were also never questioned before the need of a vocational licence, which allowed haulage companies to place enormous pressure upon drivers and exploit them to work incredibly long hours. Of course, a driver in the 1970's earned more money by delivering to as many destinations as possible. Either way fatigue was inevitable. With little sympathy from employers accidents involving HGV's grew year on year, and the health of drivers begun to deteriorate.

To help towards combating driver fatigue haulage companies started to purchase trucks with sleeper cabs – a built-in bunk fitted behind the driver. First of which has caused a few arguments as to whom was the first truck manufacturer to introduce diesel-powered large trucks with a sleeper cab. And although AEC and Leyland are certainly strong contenders, one of the first successful truck manufacturers to introduce sleeper cabs to British roads was the Swedish company – yes, you guessed it – Volvo, in particular the F88 model in 1965.

Now truck drivers had a purpose built vehicle to sleep in, allowing them to be on site – as it were – 24/7 ready to collect the next load for delivery after a nights (or days) rest. And drivers that sleep (basically live) in their trucks throughout the week became known as trampers. Unscrupulous hauliers continued to put drivers under increasing pressure to catch an early load or make that last delivery on time, so accidents caused by HGV's continued to grow, regardless of having a sleeper cab to rest.

Transport managers increased their exploitation of drivers by encouraging them to find their own loads on return journeys if the haulage company didn't have any planned. For some drivers the independence was like working for themselves, and it saved transport managers finding extra loads (back loads). As they saw it, if the wheels turn they earn. But if they weren't earning drivers soon found themselves finding work elsewhere.

Some haulage companies soon became national, such as BRS (British Road Services), and had depots across the country. A driver could call into the nearest depot after doing a delivery, where he could pick up another ready-loaded trailer, or even a completely different truck for his next delivery.

The early days of trucking, especially with articulated vehicles, included general haulage using flat bed trailers. But many companies receiving heavy goods didn't have forklift trucks to unload them. Loads had to be manhandled or craned, if available, for heavier loads. Gradually, as more and more companies purchased forklifts, manhandling loads became less and less. And before curtain-side trailers, rope and sheets secured and covered loads to keep out the weather.

Tying down a load became an art in itself, using special knots such as the dolly-knot or clove-hitch knot for tightening ropes and prevent load movement. With different size and shapes of loads that needed covering, roping and sheeting properly could only be gained with experience, and most truck drivers took pride in their sheeting methods.

Once sheeting and roping was complete the load must be constantly watched through the rear-view mirrors, looking at the trucks profile through shop windows or if driving an articulated vehicle as it turned or going around a bend. Not forgetting frequent stops at roadside cafés, although that may be just an excuse for a cup of tea and a bacon sandwich. However, wet weather caused natural-fibre ropes to shrink and tighten. But once dried they stretched back and loosened allowing the load to move. So it was worth stopping to check if the load remained secure.

Whether travelling to the docks to fetch a container, trunking up and down the A1 or tramping through the week, the exploitation of driver's hours were still a huge national problem. In 1960 the government introduced the requirement of all HGV drivers to log or record their start and finish time, starting and finishing place, the hours worked, rest periods and daily mileage, which can then be monitored by the Ministry of Transport.

The log sheet came as a block of unnumbered forms where after each shift one completed sheet was ripped off and handed to the transport manager. Trampers retained all their sheets until they returned to the depot. All log sheets had to be kept by the haulage company for twelve months. The daily recordings were supposed to be a truthful record of a working day as there were rules to adhere to, supposedly designed to safeguard the driver and road safety.

The various entries for work, driving and rest periods had to be recorded as the day progressed. But more often than not, due to log sheets having no identifying numbers, daily work, driving and rest periods could be changed or fiddled (more so the case) to comply with the new regulations. Drivers regularly did this to ensure they got home or late for a delivery due to traffic jams and hold-ups. This was usually done by starting one log sheet and then towards the end of the day screwing it up and writing another to reflect an honest working day.

The new HGV regulations also gave the Ministry of Transport authority to pull over drivers at any time of the day or night to check their log sheets. If found failing to complete a log sheet through the progression of their working day, more often than not a fine would be imposed. For persistent offenders a spell in front of the judge awaited with a higher fine, or a licence revoked, or both. But drivers were rarely caught.

The word soon got around of a Ministry check-point where drivers signalled each other by flashing lights, sounding a horn or waving a log sheet out of the window. If the approaching driver had anything to hide regarding his log sheet, he could then stop and complete it to suit his day's work before proceeding if he felt he might be checked.

By 1970 the Ministry of Transport had ten years of data to use for developing tighter rules. So the introduction of a 'logbook' was introduced at the same time the compulsory HGV driving test became law. The new logbook was basically similar to the layout of the old log sheet, but it now had a sequence of issue numbers printed on them to show if a driver had defaced or completed a different log page that didn't run in number sequence.

The haulage company also had to sign for any issued logbooks, in turn the driver had to sign for receipt of each issue, only to return it to the office completed, signed, and without any pages missing. But naughty drivers and haulage companies were quick to discover loopholes.

It wasn't uncommon for haulage companies and drivers to carry a second logbook for obvious reasons. The scam allowed a driver to work a full day under one logbook, only to continue working and driving through the night using the second book. And if pulled by the Ministry or a haulage company being paid an uninvited visit, the offender(s) would have a phantom logbook showing a law-abiding record. The deception was finally discovered when a driver fell asleep at the wheel and inevitably crashed the truck.

Within a few years speed restrictions were also introduced, where motorways now had a national 70mph limit. Although HGV's were restricted to 40mph on single carriageways since the early 1960's some trucks at the time could actually exceed 70mph and continued to do so on all roads. And a log sheet or logbook doesn't know how fast a vehicle is travelling. Something had to be done to stop speeding trucks and the continuous logbook scams, so in 1975 a new system was on the horizon – the analogue tachograph device.

Chapter 5

INSPECTIONS, CALIBRATIONS, RULES AND REGULATIONS

MOT: HGV's were generally ignored when it came to vehicle road safety until the introduction of the MOT (Ministry of Transport) test for road vehicles as per the Road Traffic Act 1956. At first it was nothing more than a road-worthiness check of steering, brakes and that all lights on the vehicle worked. The test was also originally for vehicles over ten years old, taken every year thereafter.

A ten year old vehicle, however, especially in the 1950's and 1960's were merely rust buckets, so many failed the simple test. The government quickly introduced an MOT for vehicles older than seven years in 1961, and in 1962 introduced a test for commercial vehicles. In the same year a valid MOT certificate was required to buy a road fund licence – a tax disc – for all road vehicles.

The Ministry of Transport continued to introduce more and more specifications and in 1968 these included an annual test for tyre wear, windscreen wiper condition and washer serviceability, exhaust system condition, brake lights, direction indicators, and the vehicle horn. In 1977 chassis wear was introduced, and in 1991 ABS, front fitted seatbelts, engine emissions for petrol engines (1994 for diesel engines) and excessive wheel bearing wear.

A progressive expansion of the test continued with a deeper tyre depth requirement and a test for rear mounted seatbelts in 1992. In 2005 a computerised MOT certificate system was introduced to supersede the old written test certificate and prevent fraud. In 2012 the MOT test was, yet again, updated to predominantly prevent fraud of vehicle mileage declaration.

A plain paper certificate was introduced as nothing more than a copy for the vehicle owner's records, where the vehicle details, including present mileage, are recorded onto the DVSA database. And because all vehicle insurance companies have to log policyholder details on the database, the police can now see, and if necessary issue fines from a screen fitted in their patrol car if a vehicle doesn't carry valid documentation.

Goods vehicles qualified as being over 3,500 kg GVW (Gross Vehicle Weight) – the overall vehicle weight and load – and trailers over 1,020 kg unladen, or 3,500 kg GVW if fitted with overrun brakes, the MOT test is conducted by DVSA staff, or at a DVSA Authorised Testing Facility (ATF) or Designated Premises (DP) or a Goods vehicle testing station (GVTS) appointed by the DVSA.

There are also medium sized Goods vehicles – category C1 – with a Maximum Authorised Mass (MAM) of 4-tonnes capable of 80 kph (50 mph). A category C1 + E is a drawbar and trailer combination with at least 2- tonnes MAM and at least 8-metres in length, capable of 80 kph (50 mph) or a medium sized articulated lorry with a MAM of at least 6-tonnes and at least 8-metres in length and capable of 80 kph (50 mph). But it doesn't end there.

Category C vehicles (rigid) is a vehicle with a MAM of at least 10-tonnes and at 7-metres in length, capable of 80 kph (50 mph). Category C + E (articulated) vehicle is with a MAM of at least 18-tonnes and at least 12-metres in length, capable of 80 kph (50 mph). Or a category C draw-bar and trailer combination with at least a 4-metre platform length, and at least 4-tonnes MAM, suitably braked and coupled, with a combined weight of at least 18-tonnes and a combined length of at least 12-metres, capable of 80 kph (50 mph).

Although HGV's have to take the same MOT test inspections as of cars and light commercial vehicles, the additional items are enormous in comparison that include serviceability of: road wheels, nuts and hubs; size and type of tyres; side guards; rear under-run devices and bumper bars; spare wheel and carrier; vehicle to trailer coupling; trailer parking and emergency brake; airline connections; spray suppression, wings and wheel arches; cab security; cab doors; cab floor and steps; seats; security and condition of body; mirrors and indirect vision devices; glass and view of the road; speedometer/tachographs; speed limiter; pressure/vacuum warning and build up; hand lever operating mechanical brakes; service brake pedal; service brake operation; hand operated brake control valves; condition of chassis; electrical wiring and equipment; engine and transmission mountings; oil leaks; fuel tanks and systems; axles, stub axles and wheel bearings; steering mechanism; transmission; additional braking devices; brake system and components; markers and reflectors; lamps; service, secondary & parking brake performance; previous MOT plate; current speed limiter & tachograph calibration label; dangerous defects.

As you can see, additional to the main principle of vehicle checks HGV's have to go under a huge pass requirement to continue service upon British roads. HGV's also have to have a minimum 13-week safety inspection, depending on vehicle application, many of which have a 6-week inspection that are compliment with MOT pass requirements. They also have to be documented and logged as part of the vehicle's maintenance history – pass or fail – including defects by the inspector/service centre and the owner/operator to retain their Operators licence.

Trailers are also subject to a 6 or 12-week inspection, depending on application, as well as a yearly MOT that is as rigorous as the prime mover test. Parts of the trailer for testing and/or inspection include: axle(s); hubs & bearings; brakes – ABS, EBS, slack adjusters, discs, pads and calipers or shoes and drums; brake chambers; cables and airlines; floor, curtains – straps and buckles; load restraining straps; body; roof; doors – fixtures, locks, handles, hinges and fittings; bulk head; chassis; landing legs; tow (king) pin and bed; airline and electrical sockets; lights; markers and marker boards; reflective markers; hazard signs; Ministry plate on display; auxillary attachment(s) and mountings; dangerous defects.

All trailers subject to an MOT has to display a yearly Ministry test plate showing date of pass, gross and trailer/vehicle weight, length, width, axle weight limits and other details. A plate also has to be fitted for display on articulated and rigid commercial vehicles with a MAM of 3,500kg and above. Ironically, in the EU commercial vehicles, including HGV's and trailers, do not legally need to undergo periodic inspections; having only to be tested on an annual MOT.

Speed limiters: Commercial vehicles subject to speed limiters and tachographs have to be periodically checked and in-date to retain a MOT test certificate and comply by the rules and regulations to retain an Operators licence. In February 1992 category C vehicles had to be fitted with a Road Speed Limiter (RSL) and display a label or sticker providing information of the vehicles limited maximum speed. This means that a HGV limited to 52mph travelling at the national permitted maximum speed of 60mph on a motorway is, in fact, breaking the speed limit, and can be prosecuted as a result.

In November 2002 European Parliament Directive 2002/85/EC amended the original directive 92/6/EEC to extend the range of vehicles to which the directive applies for the fitting of speed limiters. The Road Vehicles (Construction & Use) Regulations act 1986 were amended to incorporate these new requirements which came into effect 1st January 2005.

From 1st January 2007 further vehicle applications fell into the amended speed limiter legislation to include goods vehicles between 3,500kg and 7,500kg MAM that were first registered between 1st October 2001 and 31st December 2004, have Euro III engines approved to Directive 88/77/EEC and used on national operations in the UK. HGV's with a MAM of 7,500kg to 12,000kg first registered between 1st October 2001 and 31st December 2004 will have to have their existing speed limitation devices re-calibrated from 60mph to 56mph to suit category C and C+E vehicles over 12,000kg.

However, it is not uncommon for hauliers to govern their vehicles to 52mph or even lower, mainly to endorse maximum fuel efficiency. Although this has been proved to be ineffective for many HGV's due to the gearbox having to work harder through excessive gear changes as it tries to keep to the low speed limit when pulling a heavy load, thus using more fuel.

If a vehicle has, or is required to have a speed limiter fitted, then it is not permitted to use the outside lane of a three or more lane motorway. If the vehicle is required to have a speed limiter fitted but it is not working, it is illegal to use it on the public highway under the Road Vehicles (Construction and Use) Regulations 1986.

Tachograph tests and calibration: The tachograph, invented by German Max Maria von Weber in 1920, was originally introduced for the railroads. It wasn't until they were first introduced to road vehicles in December 1952 by the Verkehrs-Sicherungs-Gesetz (German Traffic Safety Law), making it mandatory for all commercial vehicles weighing over 7,500kg to fit them. It took a further 27 years until they became mandatory in the UK on 1st July 1979, replacing the driver's logbook System, although some were fitted as early as 1975.

Regardless of analogue or digital tachograph systems fitted to vehicles, the rules and regulations using them are pretty much similar. A tachograph is a device fitted to a vehicle that automatically records speed, distance and driver's activity from a choice of modes: other work (cross hammers symbol), drive (steering wheel symbol), rest (bed symbol) and POA – Period of Availability (cross in a square symbol).

On a digital tachograph the drive mode is activated automatically when the vehicle is in motion, and modern tachographs are supposed to be set to switch onto the other work mode when the vehicle stops. The rest and POA mode have to be manually selected by the driver whilst stationary, but in whichever mode selected, the drive mode symbol applies as soon as the vehicle moves.

Analogue tachograph is a device that is connected to the gearbox via a sender unit that picks up the vehicle movement and speed through the tachograph head that records the modes through a stylus by scratching them onto a disc-shape card. If the tachograph is a digital device the same principle applies but instead of a disc-shape card being placed into the head, the driver's working day is recorded onto a paper receipt activated by the driver's personal digital driving card containing a microchip with flash memory.

Digital driver cards store data for up to 28-days driving, which are usually downloaded by a transport office after each shift. From 1st May 2006 the analogue tachograph was replaced with the digital device so to phase out analogue recordings by 2016. Therefore, all relevant vehicles manufactured since 1st May 2006 with a MAM of above 3,500kg MAM must be fitted with a digital tachograph.

Similar to having a vehicle that requires a road speed limiter, those that have a tachograph fitted are also obliged to periodic test and calibration. And like a RSL sticker or label, a sticker has to be displayed – on the tachohead for analogue devices and inside the cab frame door aperture for digital devices – that display a current calibration date. Failure to comply the driver and 'O' licence holder can both be prosecuted and even have the vehicle taken off road in the form of a prohibition notice submitted at source by the DVSA or the police.

Operator licence: Commonly known as an 'O' licence, is required by law to own and use a commercial vehicle for commercial gain. In other words, be it a one-man band owner driver or a fleet manager of a haulage company, an 'O' licence is needed to carry goods connected with any trade or business if a vehicle is used on a public road with a MAM of more than 3,500kg or without a Ministry plate weighted more than 1,525kg. This includes owning a commercial vehicle under an agreement for hire, hire purchase, or loan.

An Operator licence can be issued in one of three formats: restricted, standard national and standard international. To carry own goods in course of a trade or business a restricted licence is required. Carrying goods for other people, for hire or reward with a restricted licence is prohibited, otherwise a fine could be ensued and loss of the licence.

A standard national licence allows a commercial vehicle to carry own goods and for other people, for hire or reward. Even if goods carried on occasion, a standard licence is still required. A standard national licence allows trailers to be collected from ports but not to be used abroad.

A standard international licence rewards the operator as a standard national licence but with the added permission to use commercial vehicles and trailers on international journeys. An international licence also includes community authorisations, which are required for all hire or reward operations in or through European Community countries. It replaces the need for community permits, bilateral permits between member states and permits for transit traffic through the EU but not permits for travel to or through non-EU countries where these are still required.

To apply for a licence you need to complete an application form (GV79). The completed form, with the appropriate application fee, must be sent to the Traffic Area Office (TAO) located in a local geographical area so to recognise where the business applicant will keep their vehicles in its operating centre when in use or at rest.

If an application is operating in between TAO's the applicant will have to check with one of them to find out where the form should be sent. Once an application has been submitted the prospective applicant must then advertise their application in a local newspaper circulating in each place where they are applying to have their operating centre(s). This allows anyone that owes or occupying buildings or land in the vicinity of the operating centre an opportunity to make a representation against an application on environmental issues.

If an application for a new licence, or for a variation to an existing licence, involves the transfer of an existing operating centre currently on another operator's licence, and the other operator is giving up use of that operating centre and is not shared by other operators, it may be possible not to have the need to advertise providing it is used under the same terms as the existing licence holder.

It is recommended an applicant should register their request for a licence at least nine weeks before the date when the licence is needed. This allows time for the Traffic Commissioner to make any enquiries. In the meantime, an applicant cannot operate their vehicle(s) until the licence is issued, unless a reasonable request is submitted, in writing, to the Traffic Area Office giving reasons as to why it's needed urgently. And saying you're busy is not an accepted reason.

The Traffic Commissioner may issue an interim licence, but can only do so if it's for a full standard national licence. A fee will also be charged for the issue of an interim licence and for each vehicle specified for use. When the fee is paid a vehicle identity disc will be sent to display in the windscreen.

When a licence is issued, it authorises a maximum total number of vehicles and, if applicable, trailers, including semi-trailers. The number applied for should take into account the number of vehicles intend to use straight away and allow for some extra motor vehicles to cover increases in business and emergencies, such as breakdowns. Under the system of continuous licensing introduced on 1st January 1996 a licence issued is for the life of the business, unless operated outside the terms of the licence, surrendered or fail to pay the required fees to keep the licence live.

A Traffic Commissioner can take disciplinary action at any time to curtail, suspend or revoke a licence if a failure to pay the required fee on time. Also to review the suitability of the operating centre(s) every 5 years. And if a new operator centre is required, a new application has to be filed and a nine-week process starts all over again.

To keep an O' licence there has to be satisfactory commitment to keep a vehicle and/or fleet in roadworthy condition. This includes a proper maintenance facility or arrangements with a garage, and to be financially viable to keep the vehicle(s) serviceable. All applicants and operators are required to show a specified level of financial standing throughout the life of the licence.

From January 2011 the levels were set at £7,700 for the first vehicle and £4,200 for additional vehicles thereafter for a standard national or standard international licence. The requirement for restricted licences is £3,100 for the first vehicle and £1,700 for additional vehicles thereafter.

A suitable operating centre with adequate access is required for all vehicles subject to O' licence application, and a requirement to understand driver's WTD (Working Time Directive), driver hours, tachograph rules, regulations and maximum load capacity of each vehicle. In addition, proof that enough resources to set up a road haulage business and run it properly are also required. Including partners/directors in charge of transport operations are professionally competent and have one or more professionally competent transport managers. This can be the owner that also drives the vehicle(s). Managers and directors have to be of good repute, and not have filed or ever been bankrupt over a qualifying period.

Deciding operator fitness the Traffic Commissioner will take in account certain previous convictions such as vehicle overloading, defective vehicles or unauthorised use, convictions connected with vehicle plating and testing or drivers' hours. Previous convictions have to be submitted on all applications, including convictions that any partners, directors, transport managers or agents have had.

If any convictions are committed after a licence has been issued, either from the licence holder, company directors, managers or drivers, these too have to be reported to the Traffic Commissioner. Failing to do so will result in the licence possibly being revoked or most definitely suspended pending further enquiries.

CPC: To comply with all the rules and regulations a CPC (Certificate of Professional Competence) is required to retain an O' licence. A CPC has two classes: standard national licence and standard international licence. CPC grandfather rights are implemented when a green certificate (GV203) was issued by the Traffic Commissioner before 31st December 1979 stating that the holder was in responsible road transport employment under an operator's licence before 1st January 1975.

If such a certificate isn't issued, a test is required by passing the CPC examinations set by the Oxford, Cambridge and Royal Society of Arts Examinations Board (OCR), or holding certain diplomas and qualifications from professional institutes. After which the qualification then has to be submitted to the Traffic Commissioner. New rules on access to the business came into effect October 1999. The rules allowed Traffic Area Offices to carry out interim checks at five-yearly intervals to ensure that operator licence holders comply with the rules & regulations.

Weights and measures: In 1986 an EU legislation incorporated UK Road Vehicles Regulations to set the maximum permissible weights and dimensions of goods vehicles. And by 1st January 1999 the Road Vehicles (Authorised Weight) Regulations 1998 act came into effect to amalgamate the EU legislation of 1986. So HGV O' licence holders may choose to comply with one set of regulations or the other, but operating a vehicle over 40-tonnes on 6 axles is only permitted under the 1998 regulations whilst in the UK.

Yep, confusing, but it means that across the EU all vehicles now have to adhere to a weight restriction for international transport capped at 40-tonnes at a maximum length of 16.5 metres for articulated vehicles and 18.75 metres for draw-bar variations (wagon and drag). And the maximum overall length permitted for a rigid vehicle is set at no more than 12 metres. Back in Blighty, the maximum HGV weight limit is 44-tonnes with the same maximum dimensions.

The same vehicle weight is not permitted on European roads, unless specific and agreed instruction has been applied for with each European country the vehicle may pass through. And each country may have variations within its EU rules according to their road and haulage limitations.

To confuse the rules on vehicle height limits further still, EU countries have a height limit of no more than 4 metres, which is due to the maximum bridge heights on major trunk routes set in place by Hitler during World War Two. And have since remained the same due to the huge cost involved replacing all 4-metre bridges he commissioned across occupied Europe. Although many new bridges, including higher ones, have since been built, the vehicle height rule remains the same.

In the UK, however, technically there is no legal limit on how high a vehicle should be to use on the road. But HGV's must be able to pass under bridges along its desired route unhindered and without causing undue care or damage to other road users, buildings, obstacles and trees. And where upon motorway bridges are uniformed with a height of sixteen and a half feet, HGV's and trailer design must allow for this clearance of motorway bridges to forward freight. A height indicator must also be displayed in the cab and show overall height of the vehicle (including trailer/load, whichever is the highest).

When a truck drivers is stopped by the police or DVSA they must comply with any lawful instruction. Failing to do so is an offence and can lead to a separate prosecution. It is also the driver's responsibility to inform the officer requiring the vehicle to be weighed of any unusual characteristics of the vehicle or its load. This includes hazardous materials and abnormal loads being carried.

According to the Road Traffic Act 1988 if the vehicle is weighed and indicates to be above the permitted limit, the driver, operator and the consignor may be liable for prosecution. It is classed as an absolute offence, meaning that an offence has been committed even when the driver or haulage company was unaware the vehicle was overloaded. If found to be guilty, a fine of £5,000 per offence can be imposed. And per offence means each axle being found to be overweight. A prohibition notice can also be issued at source, preventing the vehicle from travelling any further from where it was weighed, leaving the driver either an expensive or long walk home.

To make matters worse, if caught driving an HGV whilst overloaded and involved in a traffic collision and/or cause injury to a third party, the driver and O' licence holder can be charged with a further serious offence using a vehicle in a dangerous condition. This also carries a £5,000 fine as well as the driver's licence endorsed/revoked and a discretionary disqualification. Not forgetting to face a hearing at the Traffic Commissioners discretion.

At first, the driver is interviewed under caution by the police or DVSA immediately following being stopped. The driver must then adhere to any instruction given, by which the driver either mentions or agrees with the location of a weigh bridge to proceed to for further investigation. And if possible produce any weigh bill/consignment notes that coincide with the load on the vehicle.

It has to be remembered that pleading ignorance is no defence when attempting any denial of driving an overloaded vehicle. And saying that the overload was purely accidental or unintentional, or outside a driver's control, will be taken down as evidence, laughed at, then used against you. Although such evidence may be useful in mitigating circumstances. But if the load were grossly overweight, no such evidence would be any help whatsoever.

To be fair to haulage companies, consignors can and do state incorrectly the proper weight of their loads by either knowingly breaking the law or, more often than not, being totally ignorant towards any Road Traffic Act. After all, they assume the driver and haulage companies know the weight of everything, because it's their job to know. So it is recommended that the haulage company, and in particularly the driver, receive in a form of creditable documentation details of the cargo weight from the consignor. Ensuring that the weight is on the weigh bill/consignment note.

In 2011 DVSA introduced Weigh-in Motion Sensors (WiMS) to catch vehicles whilst travelling on public roads. And coinciding the new technology with the Automatic Number Plate Recognition (ANPR) system, allows police and DVSA officers to specifically target overweight HGV's and lighter commercial vehicles.

HGV's travelling on motorways and A-road routes now ride over a set of piezoelectric sensors placed into the tarmac that instantly weigh the vehicle passing over it. At the same time ANPR cameras takes a photograph of the suspect vehicle when the piezoelectric sensors are triggered.

The information is then paired against the vehicle and sent to a DVSA computer in an office a few miles down the road. And if the suspect HGV is overweight the vehicle details are forwarded to an in-cab computer screen fitted in a police or DVSA vehicle that may stop the vehicle and escort it to a handy near-by weigh bridge, where upon further and more detailed checks can be carried out. Modern technology – there's no escape.

As you can see there are a huge amount of rules, laws and regulations put in place before starting the engine and turning a wheel. But the DVSA, Transport Commissioners, Department for Transport and the CMPG (Central Motorway Police Group) will be delighted to empahsise the requirements, especially when you have been either summoned before a court or a public panel with the Traffic Commissioner, or fell victim to a roadside vehicle check, or, god forbid, involved in a road traffic incident.

Seatbelts: fitted to all road vehicles, including HGV's since October 2001. But trucks have exemptions when carrying out a reverse manoeuvre, driver has a valid medical exemption certificate, using a vehicle adapted for deliveries that are no more than 50-metres apart, discovering a defective seatbelt during duty, using a vehicle on trade plates whilst travelling to investigate or to a place of repair.

Reversing alarms: contrary to belief, by law goods vehicles with a gross vehicle weight over 2-tonnes do not need a reverse bleeper or alarm fitted, including buses and refuse trucks. But EU Health & Safety regulations state that a commercial vehicle must be able to operate an audible warning system when reversing in a public place or within the confines of a business premises where pedestrians can walk behind without notice. To add even more frustration, vehicles with a GVW less than 2-tonnes such as light vans, cannot use reversing bleepers on public roads, and restricted to use between the hours of 23:30 to 07:00hrs. Or used on a road if the sound omitted is similar to that of a pedestrian crossing that are likely to cause confusion.

The outrageous and conflicting EU against UK regulations on the use of vehicle reverse alarms makes a somewhat mockery out of the very real statistics of casualties sustained at work by vehicles reversing – a quarter of all injuries, with or without the use of reverse warning audible sounding devices [2021]. There is also the same percentage of all vehicles equipment and premises damaged caused by reversing. Nevertheless, the actual fault is undoubtedly human, and it is down to training – or lack of it.

Tyres: commercial vehicles using public roads have to ensure all tyres are free from defect that may otherwise cause damage to the vehicle, road surface or injury to other road users. If it has a break, bulge, tear or cut in the wall or surface of the tyre, or has a tread less than 1mm [2021] (subject to change by DVSA) throughout a continuous band around the entire circumference measuring around at least 75% breadth of the entire tread. Vehicles less then a GVW of 3.5-tonnes have the same principle apart from the minimum legal tread depth, where upon road vehicles under a GVW of 3.5-tonnes must have a minimum tread wear of no less than 1.6mm [2021] (subject to change by the DVSA).

For all vehicles, tyres must be inflated to no more than the maximum pressure according to tyre and vehicle manufacturer recommendations and no portion of the tyre under layers, ply or cord must be exposed. In addition to compulsory driver checks, twin-wheel axles must be free of any trapped debris caught in between the tyres prior to travel.

Chapter 6

THE TRAFFIC COMMISSIONER

Traffic Commissioners have controlled the country's vehicles and upheld Her Majesty's laws of the highway since 1931. And since 1997 the government handed upon on a silver plate literally hundreds of rules and regulations specifically created for governing commercial and passenger service vehicles to Traffic Commissioners. And yet, it's probably true to say, those that are not employed or involved within the haulage or passenger vehicle industry, has ever heard of them. And for those that have, probably never realised how important their duties are or the powers they have.

There are now seven Transport Commissioners appointed by the Secretary of State for Transport covering various regions around the UK. Amongst the many duties to uphold is the awarding of O' licences, registration of local bus services and granting vocational licences, including suspending, fining and/or revoking them.

Needless to say Traffic Commissioners are one of the most powerful individuals in the UK, wearing many hats, including judge, jury and executioner to HGV and PSV drivers. Within the industry, almost without exception, they have been regarded and treated with the utmost respect. Out of earshot the affection may be very much different, in particular from those that have been summoned before them.

They are statutorily independent in their licensing functions, and when necessary they chair public inquiries when considering environmental suitability of HGV operating centres and the possibility of disciplinary action against operators that have not observed the conditions of their licences. The Senior Traffic Commissioner has important responsibilities to determine how their Traffic Commissioners perform their statutory functions. This includes determining which statutory functions each Commissioner works on, and issuing general direction and guidance to the Traffic Commissioners and Deputy Traffic Commissioners (DTCs). Their mission is to champion safe, fair and reliable passenger and goods transport.

Although on a mission they also represent a modern approach to regulation, ensure the fairness of individual licensing decisions, work with transport groups to improve safety, competition and the reliability of road transport. Use their powers to ensure that O' licence holders operate the types of vehicle they're entitled to, including that they are reputable, competent, and adequately funded. Encourage all operators to adopt robust systems so that there is fair competition.

If required they can impose financial penalties against bus companies that fail to run registered local transport services on time, impound vehicles for operating illegally and either include further penalties or decide if the vehicle should be returned to the operator. Consider the fitness of vocational drivers or those applying for a vocational licence based upon their conduct. Asked to impose traffic regulation conditions to prevent danger to road users and/or reduce traffic congestion and/or pollution. When they decide a case at a public inquiry they act in a judicial capacity to ensure proceedings are fair and free from any unjustified interference or bias.

Traffic Commissioners tend to work independently from the Department for Transport (DFT), which allows decisions to be open and transparent. And whilst they have responsibility in their area for the licensing and registration of HGV and PSV operators, they delegate a great deal of their work to the Driver and Vehicle Standards Agency (DVSA).

Some may say they abuse their power to the point of bullying truck and bus drivers with random road-side checks, just because they can. Far from it. They work closely with other DFT officials to ensure they have the level of support needed to undertake their qualified functions.

Committing a Road Traffic Act whilst holding a vocational licence, be it major – driving whilst under the influence of alcohol, or minor, speeding at 52mph in a 50mph maximum restriction – the police have to report every offence to the Traffic Commissioner. Even when in charge of driving a private vehicle – including a bicycle. A somewhat controversial rule considering those that qualify only a car licence are mainly forgiven by police with a caution when committing the same or similar minor offence.

Whether or not the Traffic Commissioner decides to act upon the offence, and if the offence allows the endorsement of penalty points and/or a fine, which is most of the time, then a hearing will be arranged. The driver committing the alleged offence, as well as the O Licence holder/operator, will then be summoned before a panel of HGV hating officials, allowing them to scorn over the driver and operator before reaching an inevitable decision – death by hanging. Well, not exactly that harsh. But it will be the closest punishment they can lawfully hand down.

The letter calling an operator or applicant to the inquiry, commonly known as the 'calling in letter' explains why a Public Inquiry has been called and gives details of the legislation that it has been called under, together with the evidence that the Traffic Commissioner will consider. If the operator or applicant is part of a company partnership, the other partners should attend the inquiry. In the case of a company, at least one director or a senior representative with written authorisation from the board of directors, will need to attend to represent the company at the PI. Failure to attend the inquiry could result in the Traffic Commissioner determining the case in the absence of the applicant or operator.

Evidence is not given under oath, but witnesses are expected to tell the truth as a failure to do so could lead to an adverse finding on fitness or repute by the Traffic Commissioner. The hearing is open to members of the public and any other interested parties, so be sure to see many Malcolm's and Margaret's (will explain them two later) in the public gallery gathering gossip. The Traffic Commissioner will consider, upon request, whether to hear certain sensitive evidence in private session, such as financial or personal medical information – much to the annoyance of Malcolm and Margaret.

Everyone who is entitled to give evidence make submissions or representations will be given the opportunity to speak and ask questions. Anyone giving evidence to the PI can expect to be asked questions by the operator or representative and the Traffic Commissioner. Proceedings will be recorded so that a transcript can be produced should one be required, which are ordered only in cases where there is an appeal against the Traffic Commissioner's decision. The 'calling in letter' will advise on what the Commissioner specifically wishes to consider at a particular hearing, where there are certain mandatory requirements for different types of licence.

The standard of proof before a Traffic Commissioner is less than that required by a criminal court. Traffic Commissioners need to be satisfied that the facts have been proved on the balance of probability. In other words, more likely than not. Parties will usually be informed of the outcome of the PI on the same day, confirmed in writing within a few days, unless the Traffic Commissioner reserves the decision. In which case the written decision will be sent to the operator as soon as possible, usually within 28 days.

The Secretary of State cannot exert control over judicial functions but Traffic Commissioners are accountable to higher courts. Applicants, operators and statutory objectors have a right of appeal, set out in the statute to the Administrative Appeal Chamber of the Upper Tier Tribunal – formerly the Transport Tribunal. If the offence is deemed serious, Malcolm and Margaret will want the book thrown at the perpetrators.

More often than not the offence is minor, and although the right to appeal a decision is granted, forget it. You will lose. The hearing is conducted as a Public Inquiry, allowing more flexibility than a normal court of law to achieve a better chance of conviction simply because the public, which includes Malcolm and Margaret, hate trucks and truck drivers.

And when – not if – but when the driver and operator are found guilty, the Traffic Commissioner can then decide punishment: fines, suspension or revoking of an O' licence, instantly placing other employees that had nothing to do with the offence on the dole queue, or worse – having previous employed drivers to sign up with a driving agency.

To give an example of relevance: a car driver caught by the police for not wearing a seatbelt can either be cautioned or fined with three penalty points put onto their licence. However, the car driver can also be offered an inconvenience by attending a one-day awareness course on seatbelt safety instead of having three points endorsed.

If the same driver has a vocational licence and committed a similar offence either in their truck or own private vehicle, the driver will be fined £100, given three points, then may be summoned before a Traffic Commissioner. The offender, already fined by the courts, could face an additional fine of £2,500 simply because they have a vocational licence. The operator could also be summoned and fined, even though they may not have any professional interest with the offence.

For more serious offences such as overloading axles, unsafe loads and continuous tachograph infringements, of course the powers of the Commissioners are very much needed to keep dangerous cowboy operators and drivers off the public roads. And it is of some comfort that such drivers and operators are now a dying breed. However, it is also a shame that the same powers and similar harsh punishments and judicial decisions are predominately given to those committing minor offences where offenders have already been fined by the magistrate.

Common offences: Major offences such as drug or drink driving carry harsh penalties, and quite right too. At the moment the legal alcohol limits applied to all cases are as follows: (a) 35 microgrammes of alcohol in 100 ml of breath; (b) 80 milligrammes of alcohol in 100 ml of blood; (c) 107 milligrammes of alcohol in 100 ml of urine. [2021] A drink driver will face mandatory disqualification for a period of at least twelve-months and it is also open to the courts to impose a significant financial penalty, a period of community service or even a prison sentence of up to six-months.

Additional, where a driver found guilty of a drink driving offence that has a conviction for a previous alcohol related offence within ten-years, the minimum period of disqualification rises to three years. And once dragged through the civil courts and hauled over hot coals, the same offender with a vocational licence has to go through it all over again and face a hearing with the Traffic Commissioner. And if already found guilty for a previous drink related offence, say good-bye to your vocational licence, and most like to face yet another fine. Only the other fine will be in the thousands of pounds and your vocational licence revoked.

Non-vocational drivers caught over the limit in comparison are, for some reason, dealt a more lenient judgement. A tad strange considering the same driver is still in charge of a vehicle, large or otherwise. A typical example: A mother-of-four was caught drink-driving whilst taking her children to school. Following a row, her husband telephoned the police to warn them his wife was over the drink-driving limit with their children in the car. Police pulled her over as she left a shop after dropping off her children at school and found her to be one-and-a-half times over the limit. Worthing Magistrates Court banned her from driving for 3-years, with a fine of £215.

The punishment, although quite rightly banning the offender for 3-years from driving, the fine was pathetic. If she held a vocational licence, however, the ban would have been for a lot longer and no doubt suspended indefinitely. As for the fine, a Traffic Commissioner wouldn't hesitate in awarding a fine that will be in the £1,000's.

Speeding is by far the most committed offence, which is dealt with by issue of a fixed penalty entailing three penalty points and a financial penalty of £100 [2021]. If a case proceeds to court the severity of punishment for a speeding offence depends on how fast a driver is travelling in relation to the legal speed limit on a given stretch of road. If you are caught speeding on a regular road then you will receive between three and six penalty points and a fine up to £1,000 [2021]. However, if your speed is grossly in excess of the applicable speed limit then you could find yourself subject to a discretionary ban as well as a fine.

If you are caught speeding on a motorway then you will receive between three and six penalty points and a fine of up to £2,500 [2021]. Again, if your speed is grossly in excess of the speed limit you may leave yourself open to a discretionary ban. It is also worth bearing in mind that those caught travelling at grossly excessive speed can even be prosecuted for dangerous driving under section 2 of the Road Traffic Act 1988 and could find themselves subject to mandatory disqualification of at least twelve months or even a sentence of imprisonment. Likewise, courts can also use the new law introduced in April 2017 to fine an offender using a percentage of their weekly wage or monthly salary against a sliding speeding scale.

Like many other offences referred to under the road traffic legislation speeding is a strict liability offence, which means that unless the evidence is defective, an automatic plea of guilty will be found. Prosecutions can be based upon a variety of methods: remote detection such as GATSO, SVDD, SPECS cameras with a laser attached, and sensor operated devices such as Truevelo, as well as devices operated by police officers such as VASCAR and hand held laser devices.

GATSO static roadside box cameras are perhaps the most common type of speed camera encountered by road users, and account for a considerable number of speeding offences. It is also worth remembering that some cameras are weighted, where sensors in the road measure the weight of an approaching vehicle. And if driving an HGV above the permitted speed limit, smile, because it's taken a picture.

A popular fallacy is that GATSO cameras can take pictures of drivers travelling both towards and away. But such devices can only work where a vehicle is driving away from the camera. Because GATSO cameras capture the rear of a vehicle the registered keeper will receive a Notice of Intended Prosecution under section 172 of the Road Traffic Act 1988 requesting that they name the person driving their vehicle at the time of the offence. Failure to comply with such a request is an offence in its own right.

Road sign violations, such as going through a red light, contravening double white lines, give-way, no entry and one way signs are regularly encountered and can have catastrophic consequences, resulting in driver disqualification. In certain circumstances a driver that falls below the standard that would be expected from a careful and competent vocational driver, may face prosecution for more serious offences such as careless and dangerous driving.

Failing to comply with a road traffic sign will, on conviction, ordinarily result in a fine of up to £1000. Where, however, the sign in question is a 'Stop' or 'No Entry' sign then penalty points can also be imposed and a driver can even be disqualified from driving. It is worth remembering, especially when driving a HGV, if a bridge is damaged the said vehicle will not be insured, therefore the operator will not be insured for any damage caused to vehicle or bridge. This is due to the three warning signs notifying a driver approaching a bridge of its height/width/weight restriction and therefore the driver should know not to attempt to drive under or over a restricted bridge as the driver should be aware of the weight/width and height of the vehicle.

It is also worth remembering that there will be a full investigation with an introduction of a preliminary investigation cost no less than £160,000 [2021] payable by the vehicle owner (unable to claim on an insurance policy). And that's before any repair costs are applied, which can also run into the hundreds of thousands. If the driver is found guilty and prosecuted, the driver and operator will face further fines by the civil courts as well as imposed by the Traffic Commissioner.

Prosecutions for contravention of road traffic signs are technically complex and strict requirements require to be met by the Crown before they can seek a conviction. Any signs, wherever they are placed, must comply with the Traffic Signs Regulations and General Directions 2002 act, that set out precise requirements in relation to the size, colour and placing of road traffic signs.

If the Crown fails to establish that these requirements have been met, a driver will have a defence to a charge under section 36 – under The Road Traffic Act 1988. Being found guilty for failing to comply with road traffic signs whilst holding a vocational licence, once again be prepared to face the executioner and an additional fine, only the one awarded by the Traffic Commissioner will be in the £1000's.

DVSA (Driver & Vehicle Standards Agency): VOSA (Vehicle & Operator Services Agency) and still commonly known as 'The Ministry' from the days of the 'Ministry of Transport,' was created from the merger of the Vehicle Inspectorate (VI) and the Traffic Area Network (TAN). Since its privatisation on 1st April 2009 officers and vehicle examiners of VOSA have been granted the ability to issue fixed penalty fines upon foreign nationals as well as UK drivers, in particularly HGV drivers.

Within the first three months of privatisation a total of £500,000 in fines were issued on drivers that included breaches of drivers hours, overloaded vehicles and mechanical defects. Even £50 fines for having an empty windscreen washer bottle soon add up. Before privatisation, and over the same period, amount of fines were almost half that before becoming independent and self-funding. Funny that.

But of course, the agency has always specified that there mission is to improve road safety by setting standards for driving and making sure drivers, vehicle operators and MOT establishments understand and follow roadworthiness standards. It simply has nothing to do with raising revenue.

By April 2014 VOSA was replaced by DVSA taking responsibility of all previous VOSA requirements, including the processing of applications for licences to operate HGV's and PSV's, operating testing schemes for all vehicles and enforcing the law on vehicles to ensure they comply with legal standards and regulations. DVSA also enforces vocational drivers working and driving hours and licensing requirements, provide training and advice for commercial operators, investigate vehicle accidents, defects and recalls, and run tests for instructors of large goods vehicles, as well as company in-house vehicle trainers.

Chapter 7

TACHOGRAPH RULES AND REGULATIONS: Zzzzzz

In a nutshell, it is the lawful duty of both driver and employer to ensure they comply with drivers' hours and tachograph rules. Breach of the rules relating to drivers' hours can result in a fine of up to £2,500. Failing to install or use a tachograph can land a fine of up to £5,000. This can apply to both driver and the employer. Deliberate falsification of tachograph records can result in up to two years imprisonment. Being convicted of serious violations of the rules relating to tachograph records can also result in the suspension or loss of an O' licence.

The rules to which a driver or employer will be subject depend upon where the vehicle is being driven at the time, the type of vehicle being driven, and the type of driving undertaken. Generally speaking where a vehicle is being driven in the UK domestic and EU rules apply. For example, under EU law a driver has to take at least half-an-hour rest after 6-hours from starting a shift, yet take into consideration driving rest periods.

So, if worked for three hours before driving, then driven for a further three hours, the driver has to take one 30-minute break before continuing driving and/or working. However, under tachograph legislation, a 45-minute break must be taken after 4.5 hours of driving. But a drivers break can be split during the first 4.5 hours by taking a 30-minute break, then a 15-minute break thereafter before 4.5 hours driving has been recorded.

If driven for 4-hours then start other work for half-an-hour, a break of at least 45-minutes has to be taken before continuing driving. So not to get confused with the incredibly EU and domestic tachograph rules and WTD (Working Time Directive) regulations each UK worker and HGV/PSV driver has to adhere. There are four main modes on old analogue and new digital tachographs used by the driver where functions are automatically recorded on a daily chart fitted in analogue tachographs or as a receipt in digital tachographs.

Other work (crossed hammers symbol): defined as work other than driving, including any work for the same or another employer, within or outside the transport sector.

POA (Period of Availability – square with a diagonal cross inside): Covers periods of waiting time, the duration of which is known about in advance. Or, accompanying a vehicle on a ferry crossing, waiting while other workers load/unload a vehicle. For mobile workers driving in a team POA would also include time sitting next to the driver while the vehicle is in motion unless taking a break or performing other work such as navigation. Drivers may not carry out any driving or any other work.

Break or Rest (bed symbol): Covers breaks in work and daily or weekly rest periods. Drivers may not carry out any driving or any other work. Break periods are to be used exclusively for recuperation. During a rest period a driver must be able to dispose freely of his time.

Driving (steering wheel symbol): Driving mode that will automatically change from any other mode as soon as the vehicle is in motion. UK vocational drivers are permitted only to work (including driving hours) a maximum of 60-hours per week as per the EU WTD rules [2021]. Drivers who are subject to the EU rules on drivers' hours and tachographs normally have to also comply with the rules on working time as laid out in the Road Transport (working time) Regulations, which were brought into force on 4th April 2005.

After a driving period of no more than 4.5 hours a driver must immediately take an uninterrupted break of at least 45-minutes. A break is any period during which a driver may not carry out any driving or other work and which is used exclusively for recuperation. A break may be taken in a moving vehicle, provided no other work is undertaken. Alternatively, a split break during a permitted 4.5 hours driving period can be replaced by one break of at least 15-minutes followed by another break of at least 30-minutes. These breaks must be distributed over the 4.5-hour period.

The maximum daily driving time is 9 hours: Example. Driving 4.5 hours – break 45-minutes (or split totalling 45-minutes) – driving a further 4.5 hours. The maximum daily driving time can be increased to 10 hours twice a week: Example. Driving 4.5 hours – break 45-minutes (or split totalling 45 minutes) – driving 4.5 hours – break 45-minutes – driving 1 hour. Or, driving 2 hours – break 45-minutes – driving 4.5 hours – break 45-minutes – driving 3.5 hours.

Daily driving time is the total accumulated driving time between the end of one daily rest period and the beginning of the following daily rest period, or the total accumulated driving time between a daily rest period and a weekly rest period.

Driving time includes any off-road parts of a journey where the rest of that journey is made on the public highway. Journeys taking place entirely off road would be considered as 'other work'. For example: any time spent driving off road between a parking/rest area and a passenger-loading area prior to travelling out onto a public road would constitute driving time unless the mode is manually changed on the tachograph. But as soon as driving commences on the public road, driving time should then be recorded. The maximum weekly driving limit is 56-hours, with a maximum of no more than 90-hours over a two-week period. For example:

Sun Weekly rest
Mon 9 hours' driving
Tue 10 hours' driving
Wed 9 hours' driving
Thu 9 hours' driving
Fri 10 hours' driving
Sat 9 hours' driving
Sun Weekly rest

Total weekly hours = (4 x 9) + (2 x 10) = 56.

So the maximum driving hours allowed over the second week period will be no more than 34-hours. A fixed week starts at 00.00 on Monday and ends at 24.00 on the following Sunday.

A driver must take a daily rest period within each period of 24-hours after the end of the previous daily or weekly rest period. An 11-hour (or more) daily rest is called a regular daily rest period. A rest is an uninterrupted period. Time spent working in other employment or under obligation or instruction, regardless of the occupation type, cannot be counted as rest, including work where you are self-employed. Example 24-hour period: Driving + other work + breaks = 13 hours. Regular daily rest 11-hours. Alternatively, a driver can split a regular daily rest period into two periods. The first period must be at least 3-hours of uninterrupted rest and can be taken at any time during the day. The second must be at least 9-hours of uninterrupted rest, giving a total minimum rest of 12-hours.

Or, 24-hour period: Driving + other work + breaks = 8-hours. Rest 3-hours. Driving + other work + breaks = 4 hours. Rest 9-hours. A driver may reduce his daily rest period to no less than 9 continuous hours, but this can be done no more than three times between any two weekly rest periods. A daily rest that is less than 11-hours but at least 9-hours long is called a reduced daily rest period. Or, 24-hour period: Driving + other work + breaks = 15-hours. Reduced daily rest 9-hours. When a daily rest is taken, this may be in a vehicle, as long as it has suitable sleeping facilities and is stationary.

To summarise, a driver who begins work at 06.00 on day 1 must by 06.00 on day 2 at the latest have completed either a regular daily rest period of at least 11- hours. Or, a split regular daily rest period of at least 12-hours or if entitled, a reduced daily rest period of at least 9-hours. Regular daily rest: A continuous period of at least 11-hours rest. Split daily rest period: A regular rest taken in two separate periods – the first at least 3-hours and the second of at least 9-hours. Reduced daily rest period: A continuous rest period of at least 9-hours but less than 11-hours.

A reduced daily rest period of 9-hours, or a split daily rest period of 3-hours then 9-hours later in the same working day are purely at the drivers discretion, and by no means enforceable by the employer. Split and reduced daily rest periods are purely a flexibility option between the driver and employer should it suit both, and not only the employer. Any other times the driver can take a daily rest period of 11-hours. Unless you work for an agency, where they believe they own you, and have the right to tell you when your next assignment will be, which more often than not, starts just after your 9-hour rest period for your whole working week.

Multi-manning is the situation where during each period of driving between any two consecutive daily rest periods, or between a daily rest period and a weekly rest period, there are at least two drivers in the vehicle to do the driving. For the first hour of multi-manning the presence of another driver is optional, but for the remainder of the period it is compulsory. This allows for a vehicle to depart from its operating centre and collect a second driver along the way, providing that this is done within one-hour of the first driver starting work. Vehicles manned by two or more drivers are governed by the same rules that apply to single-manned vehicles, apart from the daily rest requirements.

Where a vehicle is manned by two or more drivers, each driver must have a daily rest period of at least 9 consecutive hours within the 30-hour period that starts at the end of the last daily or weekly rest period. Organising drivers' duties in such a fashion enables a crew's duties to be spread over 21-hours.

Those that are a member of HM Reserve Forces, including the Territorial Army, RN Reserves, RauxAF, and RM

Reserves that drive a HGV such as recovery mechanics in the REME, there are now EU concessions. It applies to a maximum of 15-days annual camp and 10 weekend training sessions per year, giving a total of 35-days.

Weekend training is not allowed to take place on consecutive weeks – other than in respect of 15-days annual camp. A regular daily rest period of 11-hours must be taken between the end of weekend training and start of work for any civilian employer. In turn, a weekly 45-hour rest period must be taken no later than the end of 6th day following a period of weekend training. Yep, a tad confusing.

Other parts of the world disagree with the EU and its WTD. In Australia drivers of articulated trucks with a gross vehicle weight greater than 12 tonnes must take a rest period for 30 minutes every 5-hours, and rest for 10-hours for every 14-hours worked, including driving and other duties. After a total of 72-working hours a driver must spend 24-hours away from the vehicle. Truck drivers must also complete a logbook documenting hours and kilometres spent driving.

In the USA driving time may not exceed 11-hours of actual driving after a 10- hour rest period, and drivers are not allowed to exceed 14-hours overall duty after a rest period, even if they aren't driving for part of this time.

Drivers are also limited to driving no more than 60-hours in any 7-day period or 70-hours in any 8-day period. After which, a driver must take 34 consecutive hours rest after a minimum of 60-hours driving in any one working week period so to start a fresh working driving week over a 7 or 8 day driving period. These rules apply only to the hours a driver is operating a commercial vehicle. The same driver is permitted to drive either a personal vehicle or other non-commercial vehicles during this time, without being in violation. See, easy.

Digital tachograph: The digital tachograph system succeeded the analogue system as a result of European Union regulation 1360/2002 that made digital tachographs mandatory for all relevant vehicles manufactured after 1st August 2005. Digital tachographs would be required as of 1st May 2006 for all new vehicles for which regulation VO(EWG)3820/85 applies, as is published in the official newsletter of the European Union L102 from 11th April 2006.

Digital tachographs work by storing digital data on a hard drive and the driver's smart card. Transport undertakings must periodically download data from the digital tachograph (known as the Vehicle Unit or VU) within every 56-days and from driver smart cards no later than every 28-days to analyse the information and ensure that rules have been complied with.

A digital tachograph system consists of a sender unit mounted to the vehicle gearbox, the tachograph head and a digital driver smart card. The sender unit produces electronic pulses as the gearbox output shaft turns. These pulses are interpreted as speed data by the head. The sender unit and head are electronically paired and the pulses from the sender to the head are encrypted, therefore deterring tampering by intercepting or replicating the pulse signal in the intermediate wiring.

It is a legal requirement for a digital tachograph-equipped vehicle driven in scope of EU rules that the driver must use a driver smart card. If the vehicle is used without a card being inserted, the system will not prevent the vehicle from being driven, but the VU will record the fact that the vehicle has been used without a card. And it is a requirement set by Traffic Commissioners that a vehicle complying to such regulations must be able to account for all mileage gained within the vehicle.

Drivers may only be in possession of one driver's smart card, and must never use anyone else's card or allow another driver to use their card. When driving a vehicle that is equipped with a digital tachograph, drivers should ensure that the instrument is calibrated by inspecting the calibration plaque or interrogating the instrument; ensure that their driver card is inserted into the correct slot (driver in slot 1, second driver in slot 2) from the moment they take over the vehicle, and that it is ready for use, before the vehicle is moved.

The driver must also ensure the VU records the country in which they begin and end their daily work period. This must always be carried out at the time of the start or end of the period, even if the card is not to be withdrawn or inserted.

Drivers using digital tachographs also have to carry two print rolls – either left in the cab or in their driver bag - so that a printout can be produced at an enforcement officer's request; ensure that all duties conducted since the driver smart card was last removed from a tachograph are manually entered onto the printout using the manual entry facility on the tachograph; the tachograph is working properly; ensure that through the daily working period the mode button is used correctly to record other work, periods of availability, rest and breaks; protect the card from dirt and damage; use only their own card to record driving and other activities;

ensure the card is not removed from the tachograph during the working day unless otherwise authorised.

The rules are not specific on who can authorise removal of the card, but cases where cards can be removed include a change of vehicle or where another driver will be using the vehicle during a break or rest period; on multi-vehicle use in any given shift pattern; when driving is taken over by another driver; able to produce at the roadside when requested by DVSA or a police officer.

UTC (Universal Time Co-ordinated) – the time set on a digital tachograph. The internal clock of a digital tachograph is set to UTC. The time displayed on the clock face can be set by the driver either to local time or to UTC. However, all data will be recorded by the VU on the time set by the integral clock, which operates on UTC – this is the same as Greenwich Mean Time (GMT). You will need to remember that UTC is one-hour behind British Summer Time (BST). So between 01.00 on the last Sunday in March and 01.00 on the last Sunday in October drivers must account for the difference when manually inputting activity details in the digital tachograph.

For example, if drivers carried out other work for two hours between 06.00 and 08.00 in June before taking over the vehicle, they must enter this as between 05.00 and 07.00 in UTC time. As mentioned above, it is possible for drivers to set the display time on the VU to local BST, but this will not prevent the VU recording in UTC. Therefore, it is recommended that drivers leave the display time in UTC as a reminder of the difference. A digital tachograph offers the ability for a driver to enter activities carried out by him away from his vehicle.

A manual written record will only be necessary if the equipment or smart card malfunctions. If for any reason the tachograph does not make an accurate record of activities, e.g., if the driver inadvertently makes an incorrect manual entry in a digital tachograph, or fails to correctly operate the mode button or switch, it is strongly recommended that the driver makes a manual tachograph record. This is applied by signing the printout for the relevant period with a note giving details of the error and reason at the time the error is made. For analogue equipment, the record should be made at the back of the chart.

Analogue tachograph recordings are made by a stylus cutting traces into a wax-coated chart. Three separate styluses mark recordings of speed, distance travelled and the driver's activity (known as the 'mode'). The inner part is used by the driver to write details of his name, location of start of journey, end location, date and odometer readings. The reverse of a tachograph chart contains an area for recording manual entries and details of other vehicles driven during the period covered. Other than the difference of recording the drivers working day, both digital and analogue tachographs have to comply with tachograph rules and regulations, as does the driver.

Unforeseen events: Provided that road safety is not jeopardised, and to enable a driver to reach a suitable stopping place, a departure from the EU rules may be permitted to the extent necessary to ensure the safety of persons, the vehicle or its load. Drivers must record all the reasons for doing so on the back of their tachograph, printout or temporary sheet at the latest on reaching the suitable stopping place. And a roadside lay-by is not regarded as a suitable stopping place.

It is recommended that a time of under one extra hour of driving is regarded as sufficient, but repeated and regular occurrences, however, might indicate to enforcement officers that employers were not in fact scheduling work to enable compliance with the applicable rules. It can apply only in cases where it unexpectedly becomes impossible to comply with the rules on drivers' hours during the course of a journey. In other words, planned breaches of the rules are not allowed. This means that when an unforeseen event occurs, it would be for the driver to decide whether it was necessary to depart from the rules.

In doing so, a driver would have to take into account the need to ensure road safety in the process, such as when driving a vehicle carrying an abnormal load under the Special Types regulations, and any instruction that may be given by an enforcement officer. Other causes may include severe weather, road traffic accidents, mechanical breakdowns, interruptions of ferry services and any event that causes or is likely to cause danger to the life or health of people or animals.

If one of these situations or something similar arise, they only allow drivers to reach a suitable stopping place and not necessarily to complete their planned journey. Drivers and operators would be expected to reschedule any disrupted work to remain in compliance with the EU rules. Unfortunately, it's also doubtful that the DVSA or police will believe any sob stories and still prosecute whatever the excuse. Still want to be a lorry driver? You must be board by now. Really? Okay, read on, I'll soon change your mind.

Chapter 8

THE MODERN HGV DRIVER

If you haven't been put off yet and still adamant of becoming a HGV driver, you will need to take a gaggle of theory and practical driving tests before you reach the dizzy heights of a Class one or C+E driver. Providing you already have a car licence, the next step is to gain a 7.5ton vehicle licence, costing around £1,000 in lessons and fees. That's providing your car licence already includes categories upto 7.5ton vehicles. If not, a further £1,000 will be required to gain your 3.5ton to 7.5ton driving licence.

After a qualifying period of 6-months you can start lessons to gain your category C licence, costing anything from £1,200 to £2,000 in lessons and fees. After which, and after a qualifying period of 6-month, a further £1,200 or so in lessons and fees apply to gain a category C+E (Class one) licence. The actual course is usually taken over a period of one working week that consists of trailer conversion, recognition and awareness.

HGV driving tests are designed to test the skills needed to be a vocational driver. The practical test involves vehicle safety questions, driving ability and specific large vehicle manoeuvres. The set exercises will include: S shaped reverse into a bay, braking exercise, demonstrating the uncoupling and re-coupling procedure if taking a test with a trailer. If taken in a manual vehicle, it will be required to carry out a gear-change exercise during the general driving element of the test. The road test will last about an hour and the overall test takes about 90-minutes.

Vehicle safety questions for lorries and buses are basic safety checks that a driver should carry out to ensure the vehicle is safe for use. Although some checks may involve the candidate opening the bonnet to identify where fluid levels are checked, students will not be asked to touch a hot engine or physically check fluid levels.

As vehicle technology advances more and more vehicles are being equipped with electronic diagnostic systems informing the driver of the state of the engine, fluid levels, even tyre pressures. It will be acceptable for a candidate to refer to the vehicle information system when answering questions on vehicle statistics. Candidates will also be asked five questions that will be a combination of show me/tell me concerning driving faults. These will be recorded for each incorrect answer to a maximum of four driving faults. If the candidate answers all five questions incorrectly, a serious fault will be recorded.

During a driving test the examiner will give directions that must be correctly followed, so listen carefully to instructions. Test routes are designed to be as uniform as possible and will include a range of typical road and traffic conditions. Throughout the test a professional driving manner should be adhered to. If a mistake is made or thought is made, don't worry, it might be a less serious driving fault and may not affect any test result. The examiner will be looking for an overall safe standard of driving, not perfection.

Fifteen driving faults can be applied to a test, where a sixteenth will result in a fail. However, if a serious fault is committed that is considered dangerous the test will result in a fail, or even stopped if too serious. A passenger can be taken on the test, providing they're over 16 years of age, and cannot take any part in the test. All examiners are trained to carry out the test to the same standard, so as long as a good demonstration of a standard requirement is carried out, a pass will be rewarded.

DSA (Driving Standards Agency) do not conduct tests in bad light or in adverse weather conditions for the safety of the candidate and the examiner. Another test will be arranged at no further cost, but compensation is not payable. Candidates should call the telephone number quoted on the appointment letter to check whether their test will go ahead. If the driving test is not completed for reasons attributed to the candidate or vehicle, another test will have to be rearranged at the candidates cost.

Achieving and maintaining a DCPC: According to the EU and British government statistics, HGV drivers course far to many accidents on the roads and have incurred industrial injures that can be simply avoided with extra training. And it has nothing to do with bleeding yet more money out of the trade, apparently.

Officially, the aim of Driver Certificate of Professional Competence is to improve the skills and knowledge of all HGV drivers throughout their working lives. The Directive comes in 2 formats: 1. Initial Qualification. From 10th September 2009 all applicants wishing to obtain HGV status (categories C1, C1+E, C, C+E) and use the licence on a commercial basis, will be required to complete training and 2 modular exams (modules 2 & 4) to achieve Driver CPC initial qualification.

2. Periodic Training: Between 10th September 2009 and 10th September 2014 all current drivers who drive professionally are required to complete 35-hours (5-days) of training. The 5-days can be spread over five-years, i.e. 1 day/7 hour course each year.

On 10th September 2009 all existing HGV drivers gained their Driver DCPC under Acquired Rights. However, in order to keep their DCPC after 9th September 2014 and continue to drive professionally for the following 5-years, a HGV driver must complete 35-hours of approved periodic training before the deadline. And approved periodic training can only be delivered by organisations and training providers approved by the Joint Approvals Unit Periodic Training (JAUPT). To become a commercial driver and successfully gain the driver CPC qualification you must pass the following 4 modules:

Module 1. Theory and Hazard Awareness test. 100 multiple-choice questions and 19 hazard perception clips. Instructors will provide suitable literature to prepare for this module.

Module 2. Case study questions and answers. The candidate will be shown case studies and then asked questions about them. Again, instructors can organise suitable classroom, practical training and literature to prepare for this module.

Module 3. Practical Driving Test.

Module 4. Show me, tell me questions. The candidate will be asked questions about certain topics such as load restraints and asked to demonstrate their knowledge using a ratchet strap, where the candidate must show the instructor/examiner how it works and how they would use it to secure a load.

The total cost to retain a DCPC can vary but £300 to £400 is average, where upon the qualification is required to be updated every 5-years. In order to keep Britain's road transport fleet moving, thus the UK economy flowing, 2.6 million days of approved training was needed to launch the DCPC that came into effect September 2014 for all HGV drivers. It was estimated that half of the driving population will have been left untrained by the start of 2013 and JAUPT's approved trainers will simply not have the capacity to cope with the demand.

Once again, thanks to a government hell-bent on appeasing the EU and taking terrible advice from its advisors, the UK has a huge critical short-fall of HGV drivers. The last time was in 1996 when the government introduced the need to take a separate driving test for the old Class one, replacing it with the C+E category. This means a new driver now has to take a category C test before taking a category C+E test.

The scrapping of the old HGV class tests and the introduction of having to take two new ones to gain a C+E category licence can cost a new driver in excess of £3,000. A huge cost that many simply cannot afford. And haulage companies are reluctant to pay for new drivers to take lessons and a test due to the cost and fear they will change employers offering better wages and conditions. And if an HGV driver doesn't have a valid DCPC smart card after the deadline of 9th September 2014 they cannot vocationally drive any commercial vehicle over 3.5 tonnes fitted with a tachograph.

To rub salt into the vocational driving wound it doesn't help that the average age of a HGV driver is 53-years of age. Even though the entry age for HGV's has since been lowered from 21 to 18 years of age – matching HM Forces. And as more retire early, simply because the cost of retaining their licence is expensive, including maintaining a DCPC, drivers smart digi-card and periodic medicals, new drivers are not taking their place. Not only having the same costs to retain a licence, but also the initial cost of lessons and tests to gain a HGV licence. Due to this a shortfall of HGV drivers exceeded 70,000 by 2014, and has only become worse over the past seven years leading up to the 2021 crises, exceeding a staggering shortfall of 100,000.

Mainstream media only became interested by August 2021 when it became common place for many High Street shops and supermarkets failed to fill shelves with simple foods such as bread, milk, even toilet roll. And the immediate knee-jerk reaction by mainstream media was to blame the Covid-19 pandemic and, of course, Brexit. But they were nowhere near the truth. Since the sudden downfall of HGV drivers in 1996 haulage companies and fleet managers made the situation worse by employing foreign drivers – Eastern European drivers to be exact – to fill the gap. Only this was to exacerbate the driver shortfall in 2021 when many Eastern European drivers had since returned home.

In the meantime thousands of Eastern European HGV drivers, including a large number that couldn't even read, write or speak the English language, were quickly snapped up by the increasingly desperate haulage industry. Now earning more money than they could ever dream of, the word soon spread to other foreign HGV drivers back home to get their hairy arses to the UK and earn in one day they would otherwise earn in one month back in their native country. And could you blame them? No different to the surge of British brickies migrating to Germany to fill the shortfall of building trades Germany suffered from in the early eighties to help rebuild many of its towns and cities.

Haulage contractors, fleet managers and driving agencies snapped up the new influx of much needed HGV drivers, no mater what knowledge or experience of driving on the correct side of the road, let alone the incredibly inferior driving test to gain an HGV licence in the former Eastern Bloc. After all, the industry was desperate. In fact new unregulated driving agencies suddenly appeared from nowhere: rented rooms above shops, converted garages, spare rooms, even bedrooms. And there certainly wasn't a short supply of Eastern European drivers; they flooded the market.

Eastern European drivers only really had one single access to driving HGV's in the UK and that was through the back door – driving agencies. They would take anyone. And for a lot of agencies having no formal training, experience and knowledge of the trade, nor did their new drivers, so it didn't matter. As for the agency clients, all they wanted was a supply of drivers with a valid HGV licence and having no need to employ or pay insurance for. Not forgetting to exploit the new EU driving laws because we're all friends now. Well, back then we were, sort of, maybe.

With this sudden and constant influx of new drivers the hourly rate of pay plummeted. After all, why should driving agencies pay a living wage for UK drivers when Eastern European drivers were ecstatic with earning £7 per hour? Lowering the hourly rate certainly kept British drivers away, keeping the door open for yet more Eastern European drivers not needing a living wage to pay mortgages, rent, food and bringing up children. All they needed was rent for a room or share rent with up-teen others in one house, rented out by unscrupulous landlords – the next rip-off industry cashing in on the surge in the mid to late 1990's.

All sounds terrific, eh? The transport industry was now sailing on an even keel, shops were stocked to the gills and shelves were full. Not forgetting Prime Minister Tony Blair taking all the credit for saving the country from the lack of HGV drivers – a lack fuelled by his government in the first place. But their was one small problem: a bunch of Eastern European drivers that couldn't speak or read English let loose in a 44-ton vehicle to drive up and down UK highways and byways.

It appeared that reading road signs, understanding the discipline of driving a HGV on UK roads, even the basics of the Highway Code, let alone height, weight and width restrictions, meant very little and reflected in the huge increase in damage to trucks and trailers due to bridge strikes. And not just bridge strikes. Damage to third party vehicles due to driving down narrow roads sign posted as unsuited for Heavy Goods Vehicles, driving the wrong way down one way streets, even caught driving the wrong side of single and dual carriageways.

Traffic lights, barriers, pedestrian crossings, posts, street lamps, pavements and kerbs, buildings, even sign posts warning of the hazard ahead, damaged or completely ran over, all because the driver couldn't read English and cope with driving on the left. The costs were quickly mounting into the £millions, and haulage companies had to foot the bill because of insurance companies, and driving agencies, refusing to pay. Something had to be done. Oh yes, employ UK drivers, the haulage industry said. But that idea fell on deaf ears, as many Class One drivers had since retired, and remaining Class 2 and 3 drivers couldn't afford to pay the £thousands needed to upgrade their vocational licence.

The only remaining option was to pay UK drivers a better rate than before, giving an incentive to upgrade their licence to C+E. And not forgetting a national advertising campaign to entice C+E drivers due to leave HM Forces and top up their pensions with agency driving. After all, many had already been trained to C+E qualification and had plenty of experience driving across Europe, let alone UK roads. But it was too late, damaged beyond repair. The government, agencies and the haulage industry as a whole had shit on UK drivers too many times. They were simply not to be trusted.

Don't forget, it was estimated that half of all the HGV driving population will have been left untrained by the start of 2013 according to the DCPC legal requirement, and JAUPT's approved trainers will simply not have the capacity to cope with the demand to renew them. But this second wave of an urgent need for HGV drivers was still ten years away. Until then the need for Eastern European drivers never really flouted, continuing to rise through the 1990's and well into the 2000's due to UK vocational drivers unwilling to trust the government and the haulage industry. So the damage continued, and sadly many deaths caused by incompetent drivers.

Fast forward to 2021 and the saga continued with the lack of HGV drivers, only this time the tide had completely turned. Eastern European drivers were now returning home in their droves for various reasons. Some wanting to start their own business, and more than anything else, the haulage industry lost its appetite dishing out incentives to come to the UK and take jobs away from UK drivers. But with the trade still lacking thousands of drivers the hourly rate still needed to rise somewhat to have any attraction. Otherwise former UK HGV drivers will continue to stack shelves or order pick in warehouses that offer the same rate of pay agencies gave drivers.

So the haulage industry will not only have to increase the hourly rate considerably, offer much better conditions, less hours and job security, the government will also have to ditch the DCPC to catch the attention of the amount of English speaking and reading drivers the industry desperately needs. So not the right time to holds ones breath.

Retailers said there had only been minor disruption to supply chains but backed calls for urgent government action. And director of food and sustainability at the British Retail Consortium believed the government needed to increase the number of HGV driving tests, and even provide permanent working visas to those Eastern European drivers that have returned home, thus giving a longer term solution to the crises. And Logistics UK urged the government to extend an incentive scheme for employers to hire apprentice drivers. God knows how that would work out.

Nevertheless, the government pledged to work with industry leaders to attract new drivers by simplify training and encourage people to stay in the industry. And the DVSA strived to work hard to ensure almost 1,500 HGV drivers passed their driving test every week. A new consultation was launched between government officials and the haulage industry to see if it was possible to allow learner drivers to take one test to achieve the C+E qualification.

This would streamline the process for new drivers to gain their HGV licence and would increase lorry test appointment availability. The consultation will ensure road safety is paramount and set out that drivers will still be supervised until fully qualified. So in other words go back to pre 1996 and able to take a Class One driving test without having to take a Class 2 (category 2) before hand.

The consultation also looked at allowing trainers to actually examine drivers in the off-road manoeuvres part of the HGV driving test, and look at whether specific car and trailer tests should be required. This allowed a significant increase in the number of HGV driving tests to be conducted whilst maintaining road safety standards.

Driver digital smart card: All HGV drivers now require a driver's smart card, commonly known as a digi-card. The cost of which is £50, then £25 thereafter with a renewal every 5-years. There are different types of digital cards used in digital tachographs depending upon application: company cards for operators to retrieve data regarding their employees from the tachograph head.

Data can be locked in the tachograph head to ensure the data can't be retrieved by another company should the vehicle subsequently change ownership, or in the case of lease or hire vehicles that are used by many companies during its life. Workshop cards used by authorised tachograph technicians to fit and calibrate tachographs, and to either collect and/or deliver vehicles so to ensure all mileage clocked by the vehicle can be logged and stored on the tachograph for DVSA purposes. Control cards used by law enforcement agencies such as the police and DVSA officers to retrieve all data from the tachograph head. A control card overrides any company locks put in place by operators.

All activity information is stored in the tachograph head's internal memory and simultaneously onto the flash memory chip contained within whichever digital card is inserted into the head. Speed information is also stored, but only on the tachograph head's internal memory. Speed data is stored in at least 1-hertz intervals, depending on the model of tachograph head. When either memory bank is full, the oldest data is automatically overwritten with the current data. Design specifications prevent data being altered or deleted, therefore ensuring the integrity of the data for subsequent analysis and presentation in a court case.

Data is stored as a file that can be imported into tachograph analysis software. The digital data stored by the tachograph system can be analysed by a computer and infringements automatically identified. The digital data is encrypted and can't be altered or deleted by the driver once stored on the card or in the head.

Digital information is more explicitly defined than analogue data, and is less likely to be misinterpreted. When an analogue chart is visually analysed, a margin of error is present, dependent on the quality of the recording and the skill level of the analyst. However, without a digital card reader, computer and analysis software, the data can be more difficult to interpret as it is not visually represented as an analogue chart, and requires mathematical calculations to decipher the information from its presented format.

There is no facility to record the start and end locations for each day. Only the country is permitted, except in Spain where the region may also be specified. But the lack of not being able to include a start and finish place on the print readout receipt – unlike writing them on an tachograph card – causes difficulties for law enforcement agencies in identifying some infringements.

Modern urban driving: Now you have a vocational licence proudly showing your HGV category, a shiny new digi-card, successfully qualified with an accompanying DCPC, and are old enough to drive for a company or agency, you are finally ready to drive a truck. But there are those that don't want you to. In fact, there are those that want you banned from the road entirely. Until such times, although these pressure groups are unbelievably stupid not to realise everything they use is delivered by road, HGV drivers have to suffice with the government conceding to pressure and the introduction of further vocational driver training programs, if not to discourage you from your chosen career.

According to various hot-headed and crusading campaign groups, HGVs, including refuse collection and category C1 vehicles are involved in two thirds of cyclist deaths in London. And cyclists involved in collisions with HGVs are 78 times more likely to be killed than those hit by a car, where the majority of these deaths happen after large vehicles deliberately turn across the cyclist's path, apparently. And according to the Department for Transport (DfT) the average cost of a traffic accident involving NHS, recovery, police and investigation, costs the tax payer £1.7 million for each fatality.

The London Cycling Campaign once told the Telegraph 'the data showing the far higher risk of serious injury in collisions with HGV's emphasises the urgent need for all lorry operators, especially councils, to provide specialised awareness training for drivers which is now available as part of the Freight Operators Recognition Scheme (FORS).' A scheme endorsed by former London Mayor, Boris Johnson.

What the London Cycling Campaign and Boris Johnson failed to recognise, or conveniently forgot to mention to their protest groups, was that HGV drivers in the UK now have to take at least four training programs and pass four driving tests before reaching category C+E status, partake in company driving assessments and continuous awareness training throughout their driving career. And now have to add a further compulsory DCPC training course every 5-years at the driver's expense. So it is safe to say British truck drivers are the best trained drivers in Europe, if not the world.

Cyclists, however, require no test by law, no need to pay for a road fund licence, have to partake in any road and traffic awareness programs, cycle training courses, insurance or even take an equivalent bicycle MOT to ensure a minimum safety requirement.

They use the pavement where it is supposed to be an offence to do so, continuously run red lights, rarely use signals, and many ride with poor or no lights. They slow traffic down to an almost crawl by riding two, three, four and even more abreast, cause vehicles to suddenly brake by cutting in front of them and ride past HGV's on the nearside, expecting trucks to just stop, let alone see them. And yet it's the motorist, in particular HGV drivers, persecuted by the likes of former London Mayor, Boris Johnson.

Buses, however, seem to be missing from many government statistics when it comes to cyclist related incidents. So it is with a fairytale wish that one day some knight in shining armour will realise that compulsory training and a test is required for cyclists to use overcrowded UK roads, as well as making it law for cyclists to have insurance and some sort of MOT. As for car drivers, it's about time training and a test was included for the awareness of HGV's.

Car drivers only have to pass one driving test; that's it. After which, there is no need to take further tests, unless you're unfortunate to do so due to a court decision for committing a serious driving offence. They don't even, although supposed to, update their awareness on new, updated or additional rules and regulations on the Highway Code. Where a driver with a vocational licence will not only be instantly charged and found guilty of an otherwise minor offence, they have to pay twice with an even larger fine given by the Transport Commissioner.

So it is up to the Kings of the road to categorise car drivers, and it goes something like this: Meet Gary. He drives a ten-year old battered Multi Purpose Vehicle (MPV) usually a Vauxhall Zafira, with 7 seats required for his large family. Now, Gary is only 32 years old, but because he can't keep it in his pants his wife, Tracey, insisted he bought a 7-seater. Unfortunately he can only afford to buy one on some dodgy finance provider at an extortionate rate of return, because the other half of his Hi-Viz warehouse wage pays for nappies, children's shoes, cheap cider and hand-roll tobacco.

Gary is the world's angriest driver, and that is because he is jealous of his mates driving BMW and Audi sports cars. But they paid attention at school and managed to keep it in their pants, which means they can afford a pint and go out when they like. Gary can't. He has to stay indoors, constantly moaned at for not earning enough money to go on holidays, buy their own house, or even afford a packet of tailor-made fags. That's why when you see Gary driving his passion wagon he speeds, shouts and flashes his high beam at all other drivers in disgust, fails to use his indicators, suddenly stops and takes last second moves to left or right without signalling, and always runs red lights at pedestrian crossings. But at least he managed to pass a driving test – just.

The next category is all small car drivers. The bloody lot. Be they Peugeot's, Nissan's, Kia's... the list goes on. They will always hold you up, slow down and apply brakes for no reason. When approaching a speed camera they will slow down from their maximum speed of 37mph to 30mph, no matter what the speed restriction. But by far the worst category is the Nissan driver.

It seems you do not need a driver's licence to drive Nissans. In fact, it seems that failing a driving test qualifies the right to be employed by the government and given a Nissan so to slow and even grind traffic to a halt for no reason other than piss truck drivers and other road users off because cars are now fashionably evil. Ask Jeremy Vine, he'll tell you. And the worst of the worst Nissan drivers, in descending order, are those that drive Juke's, Qashqai's, and at the very bottom, Micra's.

Outrageous lane discipline, terrible parking manoeuvres, and an incredible ability to drive everywhere at 35mph. Doesn't matter, be it through town with a 30mph limit, national speed limit roads, dual carriageway or a motorway. They will use full beam to blind on-coming traffic, use front and rear fog lights when there is no fog and the slightest threat of drizzle, yet never when it is foggy. In fact, no lights are used under any adverse conditions. And the common name of these awful drivers in their Nissan's are usually Malcolm and Margaret. They instinctively hold the entire country to ransom because they not only believe, but know they are correct and everyone else is driving dangerously.

Malcolm, of course, is in his late sixties, and his wife, Margaret is in her early sixties. Both retired, Margaret was a teacher of home economics and Malcolm had a civil service position, employed as a statistic analyst. I'm sure you now get the picture. Even those that tow caravans hate these two. To protect you from outrageous behaviour of cyclists, Gary, Margaret and Malcolm, there is a very important piece of kit all truck drivers must now posses – a dashboard camera.

The dash cam is well worth investing in, some as cheap as £20. In fact, many HGV's now have all-round cameras installed, if only to prove to the court and an astonished judge that the cyclist, Gary and Malcolm were in the wrong. They record your driving whilst providing important footage of any collision or near miss that may be reported to your boss without you realising, until you return to base. And whilst the transport manager is tearing a strip off you, or banning you from site because you're an agency driver, you can casually show the footage whilst wearing a smug grin.

Nevertheless, if you become or are already an agency driver, get a personal dash cam. Otherwise you will be 'banned from site' before you attempt to put across your version of events. It's also worth remembering that being an agency or full-time employed driver you are responsible of the vehicle you drive. So use the rules rather than fight them.

After all, they are there to protect you. And let's face it, no one else will, including your employer, and definitely driving agencies.

It's worth remembering when driving a truck you are most definitely not in a race. You can't beat a BMW M3 from the lights, let alone a Nissan. Well, okay you can thrash Nissans, but all other cars you can't, so why bother. Let them go. As for those that cut you up, you will quickly learn that a car, bus or cyclist about to arrogantly barge into your way, expect you to either stop or slow down to let him or her in your path. So let them. You will still be able to continue on your journey, and you won't be able to catch them to drag the culprit out of their vehicle or off their bike to explain the error of their ways. So why bother getting angry about it. Forget about running them over. it simply isn't worth the time, effort or court case.

Expect all road users and pedestrians with the contempt they deserve. Laugh at their stupidity, and with your dashcam, seek revenge by showing your mates the footage or submitting their crap driving on social media websites. It's much more satisfying rather than face criminal charges for beating the shit out of them, or causing you mental grief by reflecting on their twatness throughout your shift.

Expect the unexpected. A car will always try and undercut you, will approach a parked vehicle yet pass it onto your clear side of the road, causing you to slam on the anchors, even though it's your right of way. Traffic lights will change to red as you approach them. And beware of painfully slow Margaret because she will arrogantly fail to speed up as she enters onto a motorway or dual carriageway, causing you to slow down. And Malcolm will overtake you but pull back into the slow lane only to slow down to 51mph and have you slowly overtake. But Malcolm will then speed up to match your maximum speed, unwilling to allow you to pass, simply because he is a twat.

As for BMW and Audi drivers, and yes, okay, Mercedes drivers too, they will cut you up just because they have a death-wish to get in front and exit the road with only a few yards to spare, rather than throttle back and wait a few more seconds for the exit to approach them whilst safely driving behind you. And putting aside London, Cambridgeshire has the most arrogant of drivers in the UK, so be aware of their unbelievable terrifying driving habits and that they have one of the highest traffic collision statistics in the UK. Junction 24 to 28 on the A14 is testament to any statistic, so keep your eyes peeled.

Floods: Since the 1990's flash flooding on roads, including major routes and motorways, have become increasingly common. 6-inches (15cm in new money) of fast moving flash flood water can easily knock over an adult. 24-inches (60cm) can move a car. The same 24-inches can damage the engine of a large vehicle such as an HGV. If faced with driving through a flood that is deeper than the exhaust, make sure revs are continuous and don't ease or take off the throttle otherwise water will quickly enter through the exhaust and into the DPF system or even the engine.

Ensure a bow wave caused by pushing the floodwater doesn't exceed the base of any air intake, crankcase breather or auxiliary drive belts. Same applies to driving through large puddles, otherwise engine failure is greatly increased. Once past the water obstacle carefully apply brakes to test and disperse water from brake surfaces, and check air pressure gauges for any loss of pressure caused by breaking or dislodging airlines and reservoir fittings.

Driving through standing water at speed can lead to tyres, especially with poor tread depth, loosing contact with the surface of the road, known as aquaplaning. Yes, even 44-tonners. This will inevitably lead to loss of steering and braking control. To combat aquaplaning it is recommended to immediately step off the throttle and hold the steering wheel lightly, so not to fight the direction of the vehicle until it finds grip once again, which will happen quite quickly. Only then can the vehicle be brought back under control. And when safe to do so, test brakes for efficiency.

No smoking rule: Since July 2006 it is a criminal offence in the UK to smoke in any public building or a place of work with more than one employee, including company vehicles used by anyone managing or controlling it. Premises and vehicles must also display clear signage upon entry so any potential visitor, customer or employee is notified and aware of the law. Vehicles must also be smoke-free if used for the purpose of transporting passengers.

Smoking bans are enforced by local authorities, including company vehicles from where they are based, or from where an Operator licence is registered for use. Enforcement officers, including the Police and officers from the DVSA can issue fixed penalty notices, with an option to request a court hearing made within 29-days of the notice given. A fixed fee is £50 (reduced to £30 if paid within 15-days), or if the case goes to court the maximum fine is £200. And failure of a manager or controller of the vehicle to prevent further offences in the same vehicle can result in a fixed fine of £200 or a maximum £2,500 in court [2021].

Bearing in mind that caught smoking in a vehicle, HGV or otherwise, and the driver has a current vocational licence, the driver must report the offence to his manager, with or without an O' licence, whom in turn must report the said offence to the Traffic Commissioner. Failure to do so may result in further fines and/or a disqualification period of an open-ended term awarded by a hearing. Yet another great excuse for authorities to persecute HGV drivers. The law on e-cigarettes were, to say the least, unclear in 2006. As it stood there was no law banning the use of e-cigarettes as they do not produce smoke.

The anti-smoking activists were quick to respond and shouted very loudly so the government had no choice but agree with the lobbyists and bow down to their shouting by making it also illegal to use e-cigarettes in public buildings and vehicles, even though they don't expel smoke, just steam. It's no different to the temperance movement wanting to ban Kaliber because it looks like a can of alcoholic beer. Warehouse distribution centre managers were quick to allow their knuckle dragging charge-hands ban any agency drivers from site if caught 'smoking' their e-cigarette in their own cabs.

London congestion charge scheme: In other words, an outrageous cheek and pathetic excuse to raise millions of pounds out of the pocket of the motorist to be charged a fee for sitting in traffic jams. The charge, at the moment, applies to central London, although Borough councils seem to expand the boundaries as and when it pleases. The boundary is indicated by signs on the road and at the roadside displaying the congestion charge logo – a big white 'C' encircled on a red background for clear recognition. Well, when I say clear, I mean almost completely worn out it can easily be missed. But these signs are designed carefully to empty the wallet of an HGV driver.

The congestion charge of £9 was once applied Monday to Friday between the hours of 0700hrs to 1800hrs excluding bank holidays. It is now £15 every day, except Christmas day, between the hours 07:00hrs to 22:00hrs [2021] and the cost is set to rise even further, as well as becoming a 24hrs charge and the zone expanded, yet the charge hasn't made any different to traffic jams. In fact congestion has become worse ever since it was introduced 17th February 2003. Better still, simply avoid London deliveries all together.

Further to the congestion charge, vehicles, in particular HGV's now have to be within a minimum emissions category, otherwise further charges apply. And from 2016 yet another law has been introduced for HGV's to have an additional window placed in the lower part of the passenger (near side) door. Especially designed so stupid cyclist can be seen trying to undertake, on the assumption arrogant cyclists can't read the huge LED flashing 'cyclists beware' markers and the many signs and stickers that now have to be plastered over HGV's. The thousands of foreign vehicles that drive around London streets every day, however, seem to have missed that particular memo.

Telematics: IT (Information Technology) is being increasingly recognised in the haulage industry as fuel and transport costs continue to increase year-on-year. Telematics is a way of relaying computerised information from a vehicle to a control centre.

Telematic systems allow the traffic office to monitor the progress of their vehicles during journeys, when stopped, and during maintenance or repair. Sensors around the vehicle send a signal to an onboard computer then, in effect, telephones another computer at a central base, such as a traffic office, of any real time or potential problems. And not just aspects of mechanical and electronic data from the engine. Other components around the vehicle and trailer can be monitored: brakes, lights, tyre wear and air pressure can also be checked over thousands of times during a single journey. Depending which system is installed it can alert the office and driver of any hazards ahead, such as traffic jams and low bridges.

Other benefits include delivery point awareness, GPS recording, even assist the recovery of vehicle and driver in the event of theft or hijack by simultaneously sounding an alarm at source and back at base so the police can be alerted with time, grid location, driver and vehicle details in one short burst of information. And back at base the speed and location of the vehicle can be monitored on a screen, where an alarm can be triggered if the vehicle is speeding or strayed away from pre-determined routes. The downside is that you are being watched and monitored throughout an entire shift, including visually by the onboard cameras. The driver can then be either alerted (bollocked) in real time or at the end of a shift.

Every month or so new improved software programmes are developed, even hand-held devices can now be used, or advanced mobile telephones, making a quick supersession of technology from just a few years ago. And with the introduction of the digital tachograph and electronic road user charging systems, there is no doubt that telematics for HGV's are here to stay.

There's even a breath analysing device where a driver can be tested for alcohol consumption. ON the screen a nice big green tick for okay, but a red no entry sign if you fail. Oh, the vehicle won't start either, and you can't overide the system. It also records the level of alcohol on your breath and tell-tales the boss via link to a computer or even a smart phone. This system is rapidly becoming widespread and will continue to have an increase role in the future of the haulage industry, and maybe become a legal requirement for haulage companies to survive. But there is cheat you can do to fool the machine that the inventor of this gadget didn't think off. And I'm not going to tell you. Not for free, anyway.

Going the extra mile: Basic licence holders – car drivers – will definitely underestimate the skills and professionalism vocational truck drivers have had to learn to retain their licence. They have no idea concerning the different vehicle category driving tests or digi-cards or the DCPC qualification. They will also fail to recognise the countless driving assessments taken or grasp the fact that a fully laden 44-tonne articulated HGV can't stop as quick as a car.

Truck drivers will also be portrayed poorly by the media, especially when a large HGV has been involved in a road traffic incident. Or the likes of Boris Johnson and Jeremy Vine tarnishing all truck drivers with the same brush, yet has very little understanding of haulage companies. So it is down to the individual operator and driver to educate and change the perception of the industry, and help improve the overall image of the trade.

Often it's the little contributions that make the biggest difference. Think about the role of your chosen career, and how you can help customers. Not forgetting that all cars and other vehicles on the road are driven by potential customers. Or maybe they already are. Either way, the huge HGV you drive is plastered in your employer's details: name, address, telephone number, and most probably a website and email address. So upsetting a fellow road user might actually be your boss's best customer.

Meeting and greeting customers is a forgone conclusion with all businesses, but it doesn't stop at the counter or reception. The yard person, forklift driver, goods inwards and stores personnel are all representatives of customers. After all, upsetting a forklift driver can easily spread gossip and bad vibes, eventually heard by the boss, whom in turn will remember the comments when meeting his supplier – your boss – at his next meeting.

It is a well-known fact that poor customer service costs money. By not meeting customer expectations business can be effected or caught up in some messy complaint procedure. And yes, contracts have been cancelled over viscous rumours getting out of control, only for the customer change suppliers without really investigating the original problem.

Good customer service can be perceived as going the extra mile. Simply meeting and exceeding customer expectations. Avoid complaints by getting it right first time, and continuously looking for ways to improve quality. Even doing something small by wearing smarter working clothes that are clean and don't smell of body odour, or covered in oil and burger grease stains. Not wearing jeans is a good idea. And if necessary bite your tongue and walk away from potential arguments. After all, they're not coming home with you, so why bother making it worse.

Be professional at all times and prove to customers, as well as other road users, that you are a professional driver. Whatever you do, good or bad, will reflect upon you, other truck drivers and your boss, to the point of damaging the good name of the well-known brand written on the side of your trailer. Be polite at all times; a simple please and thank you is sufficient enough to sustain a good customer relationship. When visiting customer sites and warehouses, drive courteously, park carefully and correctly, always complying to site rules. And yes, even be polite to the obnoxious and stubborn security operative at the gatehouse.

Sleep Apnoea: not a fully recognised amongst truck drivers, but the symptom is getting worse, especially for those that constantly change shift patterns – through day and night journeys. Obstructive Sleep Apnoea (OSA) is a medical condition that causes difficulties with breathing during sleep. Symptoms include excessive snoring, choking and stopping breathing during sleep.

It is possible to suffer from sleep apnoea without being aware of the symptoms. And whilst asleep breathing momentarily stops many times, so the body throws itself into automatic survival mode and wakes you up gasping for air. After a nights (or days) constantly disturbed sleep, during long hours of travel up and down the highways and byways, nodding off becomes inevitable.

OSA is a symptom that is mainly suffered by name, in particularly those aged over 50-years. Other possible clues of suffering or being a potential sufferer of OSA is being over-weight. To help sufferers there are gismos available to ease the symptoms, such as nose strips that stick across the bridge of a nose, spreading the nostrils to allow better breathing through the nasal passages – much the same as anti-snoring strips. Of course, if symptoms persist, consult a doctor.

Crash bang wallop: if an accident should occur, at fault or not, first of all don't lose your temper, shout and scream obscenities or even start a punch-up. And don't admit fault, even on those rare occasions it is. You have certain legal responsibilities regarding your involvement that causes injury to others, certain animals – farm animals – damage to vehicles and property, and roadside property – lamp posts, trees, signage, barriers, etc.

Don't make a statement admitting liability or fault regarding your driving, the condition of the vehicle or road conditions. In fact, shut up. Don't say a word regarding who's to blame. Don't make any offers or promises without taking legal advice first. Don't delay in reporting the incident to the police if they aren't at the scene, which you are obliged to do within 24-hours.

Do give your company name and address, and get everyone else involved in the incident their details. Do produce documents if any other party is injured. If not carried, ensure details are forwarded to the appropriate authorities within 7-days.

Do take document details from those involved in the incident, and registration numbers, fleet numbers of vehicles involved in the incident. Do take the number of any police officer present. Do collate your own details with photographs, width of road, parked vehicles, weather conditions, time, place and date of the incident, any skid marks, vehicles involved and other damaged vehicles and/or property, signage, etc.

If supplied, open the vehicle accident pack. Some companies provide these with single-use cameras and forms to complete, including the requirement of writing your version of the incident, and with a sketch of the scene. Do contact your transport office as soon as possible. If you have a dash cam, tell the police that you have footage of the incident. This alone will be invaluable if and when a case goes to court.

Breakdown: No one wants to breakdown during a shift. But it happens. And because HGV's are what they are – they are big and tend to block roads, or at the very least slow traffic down, even on motorways. So the first thing to do should a breakdown occur is simple: don't' panic. And if it can be avoided, don't leave your vehicle in a dangerous position or obstruct the road, unless unavoidable.

Try to ensure the vehicle comes to a safe rest in a suitable place on the near side, or better still, away from the road, preferably a lay-by if possible. And switch on hazard lights if on a road. In doing so will warn approaching vehicles and minimise the disruption to other road users. If in a built-up area, inform the police of your location and what you are obstructing. And ensure to wear a high visibility (Hi-Viz) vest or jacket if you have to leave the vehicle. Do telephone your traffic office on all breakdown occasions and give them as many details as possible.

On motorways there is a different breakdown procedure: if possible stop on the near side edge of the hard shoulder. Better still, and if possible, get off the motorway at the next junction. Ensure there is enough room for breakdown and repair crews to work safely around the vehicle and switch on hazard lights. Stay with your vehicle, even if the breakdown is in a contra-flow without a hard shoulder.

Telephone your traffic office as soon as possible with as much detail of your position as possible – sign posts, countdown posts number (set at 1-km intervals) seen on the near side of the hard shoulder. Even a SatNav grid position. Details of the breakdown – puncture, wheel bearing, loss of air, brakes or even locking brakes, no lights or electrics, loss or lack of engine power, etc.

You may even see a warning icon or a code appear on the dash or screen. If it is a puncture, the transport office may ask for the tyre size. And take care climbing out of the cab on the near side to read the size on the tyre. Better still, write down the size when carrying out your daily checks before a shift starts. A flat tyre is easy to spot. Even easier to read a piece of paper from the comfort of a warm cab, rather than trying to read a half worn print on a tyre in a blizzard at night. And it will always be at night when you get a puncture. So be sure to carry a good powerful torch with decent batteries.

With a far more serious breakdown such as fire from the unit or trailer, try and stop on the hard shoulder close to the near side as possible. Switch off the engine. If the fire is too large to extinguish yourself, get out of the vehicle and stand well back in a safe area so to warn others. Call the emergency services straight away, giving details of your location, vehicle type and the load you are carrying. If it is hazardous carry out ADR emergency procedures as per your operation protocol.

Contact your traffic office and explain the situation. If the fire is out of control, and safe to do so, stop traffic approaching and keep everyone at a safe distance – motorway or otherwise. Wait for emergency services and keep your mobile telephone at hand, because there is going to be many calls coming through. With diesel or oil spillages, try and retain them from spreading to or further into the road. Water and oil simply do not mix, and skidding on diesel is difficult to avoid, particularly for motorbikes, where the inevitable will happen.

New driver's starter kit: As well as investing in a dash-cam, there are other important bits of kit a driver will need for a day or night shift. Of course, the following list isn't compulsory, or indeed mandatory, and no doubt will be added to over the years with personal requirements suited to each individual job. Over a period of time new drivers, especially agency drivers on different assignments, quickly learn what else they need on a daily basis.

A sturdy day bag such as a shoulder sports design with zipped compartments and side pockets to carry a powerful torch; pair of good work gloves (preferably leather); combi-tool or pen knife; X2 spare digital tachograph paper rolls; spare pens and pencils; black marker pen; stick of white chalk; note pads (A4 & small pocket size); A4 size clipboard folder to hold paperwork; X2 thick rubber bands or bungies and X2 bulldog clips for securing a trailer registration plate; various spare blade fuses; spare bulbs (although these should be supplied as a set already in the truck); a flask (preferably all metal); a plastic or metal 'truckers mug' c/w top; SatNav (including charger); mobile telephone charger; maps; ball of string; headache tablets; eye spray (for tired eyes): copy of the latest HighWay Code; spare batteries for electrical items; spare Hi-Viz vest; £50-£100 float (handy for nights out and toll charges); sunglasses; clean cloth/rag; windscreen ice scraper; plastic bags (for rubbish and work gloves). Other handy bits of kit include a Hi-Viz tee-shirt for warmer weather (saves wearing a vest on site); all-weather jacket; steel toe-capped boots (all sites now require the wearing of these); hard hat (some sites require the wearing of these); industrial cleansing wipes; first aid kit.

Chapter 9

DRIVING AGENCIES

Guess you already know how I feel about these places due to my experiences. Nevertheless, once you have spent thousands of pounds gaining your shiny new HGV licence, digi-card and not forgetting a DCPC card, you can now pursue your new driving career. Well, almost. There is one more obstacle – finding a company to trust you to drive their £100,000 vehicle. And the age thing is a fragile issue with most haulage companies.

Yes, technically the minimum age to drive a HGV is now 18-years of age, but for insurance purposes employers will almost certainly insist upon a minimum age of 25-years. And it doesn't end there. Many also demand a minimum of at least two years driving experience of vehicle types similar to the job applied for. And that a vocational licence is preferably clean or with a minimum of three-points.

But there is hope for newly qualified UK truck drivers and a saviour for HGV operators. Or that is what they'll have you believe. In reality they are incredible bull-shitters; the original soul shattering dream breakers and the best of the best in being shallow, careless, arrogant, selfish and ignorant – the driving agency. A recruitment agency, be it driving or otherwise, is an intermediary between its client – a business – seeking to employ someone who is looking for work. In other words, without the hassle of having to be responsible for tax and national insurance contributions, or having to offer other legal requirements such as holidays or sick pay.

The agency's secondary prerogative is to source a sucker – you – seeking work with the best suited needs of the client. The agency is sent requirements from a client to supply drivers that will suit each job description: days, nights, trampers, class reference, etc. The agency will then supply work – assignment – to its drivers suited to their application.

Using a driving agency, however, can be a useful tool in searching for a full time job. Many clients will have on-going work, where upon the temporary driver can be offered full time work after a trial period, usually after 13-weeks. This period gives the client a chance to test drive – so to speak – a potential full time driver, knowing that if they don't fit the position the client can simply ask for another agency driver without having to abide employment laws.

Payment methods for agency workers also differ. There is the option of Pay As You Earn (PAYE), the normal method of paying income tax and national insurance, no different to a regular full time employee. But there are alternatives. Umbrella companies do have their uses, offering the ability to claim travelling and fuel costs. You can also claim for meals – different tally on breakfast, lunch, evening meals and unsociable out-of-hours food – laundry, protective clothing and tools. However, thanks to former Labour Chancellor and un-elected Prime Minister Gordon Brown, a change in HMRC guidelines make it considerably harder to claim for any expenses, and they have even reduced the amount or disallowed claims on expenses that were once accepted.

Another option is to become a Limited Company. There are many accounting companies that offer to set you up as one of these, and will also look after your income tax and National Insurance contributions, charging a monthly fee for the privilege. And like an umbrella company expenses can be claimed, as well as additional costs: business calls, postage and mobile calls, paper and ink cartridges. Also hardware such as mobile and landline telephones, computers, laptops, and even vehicles can be claimed as an expense, so any VAT can be reclaimed to a degree.

Although an agency driver may be working a 12 to 15-hour shift, 5 or 6-days a week, month after month, he or she is still classed as a temporary worker. That means having very little employment rights to protect them. Often on a zero-hour contract, which is not worth the paper it's written on, a temporary worker employment rights seem to be limited with the recently introduction of holiday pay (from the agency) being the only saving grace.

However, don't expect to be successful with applying for a mortgage or bank loan, or claiming on various protection policies whilst employed by an agency. Agency employees are simply not recognised as being employed by the financial and reputable credit lending world. Even statuary rights such as maternity or paternity leave is a very grey area.

Like preying on a wounded animal, driving agencies will stop at nothing to grab the attention of vulnerable and desperate job seekers towards a temporary vacancy by exaggerating their advertisements merely to get you through the door. To give you an idea of a typical agency's lack of intelligence, the following advert, and I kid-you-not, was placed for all to see on a national job website January 2018. And they have the bear-faced cheek to ask that the applicant had an education. Here it is, as advertised, word for word:

HGV Class 1 Driver
Northampton
£32,000 - £34,000 a year
Driver position, depot Northampton junction 16, too start January it Trunking work Monday too Friday the salary is 32k a year. Normally 2 drop a day the truck 44 tonne or 7.5 tonne with container. The client is Mainly Wincanton the position is permanent work get in touch ASAP if your interested too start January.
Job Type: Full-time
Salary: £32,000.00 to £34,000.00 /year
Required education:
Secondary education

A typical generic example of a driving agency advert with a little more grasp of grammar, intelligence, and maybe walk and talk at the same time, will most probably read something like this:

We are currently seeking LGV/HGV Class 1 Drivers for our prestigious client.
The work will be delivering goods from distribution centres to various distribution centres and stores throughout the UK, will be ongoing work with guaranteed hours and various shifts over 7 days.
To be considered for this vacancy you must have a current C+E licence, digi- tacho card, full CPC and a minimum of 2 years driving experience.

You should have excellent knowledge of the tachograph and WTD laws as well as the Highway Code, and no more than 6 points on your licence with no DR or IN endorsements. All drivers will sit a driving assessment before they will be considered for work.

Rates for umbrella and limited company drivers are £12.00ph Monday to Friday day, £13.00ph Monday to Friday nights, £14.50 on Saturdays and £16.00 on Sundays.

All NEW drivers, will also be eligible for a £200.00 bonus on completion of a 20th shift (subject to tax and NI if applicable).

At first, the advert reads very well. It is informative, appears to be genuine and offers an attractive salary with continuous work, even a bonus. However, taking out the carefully chosen wording, in reality it translates to:

Although we have HGV work available, our prestigious client already has a full complement of drivers, so we are currently stocking up on new, gullible HGV drivers to exploit when finding potential customers and make us, not you, extremely rich. So come along, sign up and we will eventually offer you some work, but it will be a shit assignment no one else wants.

The work will be delivering goods from a run-down distribution centre to various distribution centres in the middle of nowhere and hard to reach stores throughout the UK. Work will be ongoing when our client feels fit, so not guaranteed. But when you do work, hours are very long and will need to cover all shift patterns.

*To be considered for this vacancy you must have a
current C+E licence, digi tacho card, full CPC and a minimum
of 2 years driving experience. Although, don't let 2 years
minimum driving experience worry you. This particular client
will take
Any new drivers, no matter how many points, because
he is desperate.
You should have excellent knowledge of the tachograph
and WTD laws as well as Highway Code, no more than 6
points on your licence with no DR or IN endorsements. But
once again, don't worry about these requirements. They're
just for the blue-chip companies we have on our books that
insist on squeaky clean drivers, so we ask for the impossible to
look good in front of our clients and rival agencies.
All drivers will sit a driving assessment before they will be
considered for work. Well,
almost all. In fact, we have many clients that aren't bothered,
but once again, we
want to appear professional to other agencies that will be
reading this advertisement.
Rates for umbrella and limited company drivers are
£12.00ph Monday to Friday day, £13.00ph Monday to Friday
nights, £14.50 on Saturdays and £16.00 on Sundays. And yes,
these rates of pay are correct, and you can earn loads of
money. I say can, because we will let you down with empty
promises of continuous work. If you're lucky you will work for
a couple of weeks, after which the work will predictably tail
off, ending up with the odd day or two per week, then maybe
the odd day every other week. Start times will also vary,
anything from 00:00 to 23:59, and not the regular times you
were promised upon signing up with us.*

All new drivers will also be eligible for a £200.00 bonus on completion on your 20th shift (subject to tax and NI if applicable). But you will never receive it because we will never have the chance of ever reaching anywhere near a 20th shift in one hit. You will be bored of us well before then, and will have moved on to other agencies, or banned from site by our clients for no particular reason, other than the traffic clerk abusing his pathetic useless power over you.

Attracted by the advert you go and sign up to pursue your dream career, but first having to prove you are legal to work in the UK and that you are a UK citizen. Yes, even UK citizens born in the UK have to prove they are UK citizens. So you must provide the following as required by all agencies:

In-date passport or a full birth certificate
Evidence of a National Insurance number – P45 or P46 but not an old wage slip
Proof of address
Two names and contact details for references
Driver Qualification CPC card (with at least 6-months remaining before renewal)
Driver's licence
Digi- card (with at least 6-months remaining before renewal)
If registered as a limited driver (own company) proof of VAT Registration certificate & Certificate of Incorporation.

And not forgetting the mountain of paperwork to complete:

Terms of Engagement for Temporary Workers
Terms of contract for services as a temporary worker

Tachograph and driver awareness test
Working hours disclaimer
Working practice disclaimer
Conduct of assignment disclaimer
Time sheet completion
Temporary worker general application form

Of course, agencies tend to differ somewhat with their application processes. But the rule of thumb is to disassociate themselves from you regarding any employment and traffic laws that maybe broken, where the agency will never admit to ever knowing of any such potential issues because you will have signed a disclaimer to prove this. So never expect an agency to support you in any grievance. They don't care and have no loyalty towards you whatsoever.

Undeterred, you sign your life away to a driving agency, and I do mean life. Any spare time you have had before will now be consumed with either sleeping – day or night, or a bit of both – and waiting for the next telephone call or text with details of your next shift. And yes, after cancelling a night out with the lads over and over again and upsetting the wife because you can't take her out or collect her from town with bags of heavy shopping, you finally receive a text message: your shift has been cancelled. And there it begins, your miserable life as an HGV agency driver.

After cursing and moaning at the agency, and being cursed and moaned at by your friends and wife for letting them down yet again, you get another text or telephone call a few days later: shift start time 07:00 Monday to Friday with a maximum 10-hours shift pattern. Great, finally some work, and it is consistent. That means you can plan your week around work, even help the wife and meet up with friends for a drink.

Oh no it doesn't, because late Sunday evening you get a text message saying that your shift for Monday is cancelled because you need to first take a driving assessment, which needs to be booked in advance with the transport department. Bit of a blow, but you can put the cancellation to good use by grabbing the chance to go to your daughters 6th Form meeting. After all, it's a chance to show an interest in your daughters education, plus the wife will be pleased because it means she can now tell her friends she can go out for the evening instead of going to yet another parents evening alone.

Monday morning arrives, and you plan your free day. By lunchtime, however, you receive another text message: assessment arranged this afternoon at 17:00. What do you do? You need to attend the assessment and prove to the company that you are a competent driver. But you have promised to help your family. Now desperate to think of a solution, you can only think of two options: either telephone the agency and explain that you can't attend or go and upset the wife and daughter.

This common occurrence has trapped many agency drivers, which can have huge consequences. Telling the agency you can't make it because of a prior family engagement will, undoubtedly, upset them. In turn they will shout and curse down the telephone, calling you all the names under the sun and that you're a waste of space, conveniently forgetting they let you down by failing to tell you about the assessment in first place. And the fact they forgot will increase suspicion of their intellect and question a considerable lack of professionalism.

On the other hand, there are many agencies to choose from, and they can't all be bad, can they? So you make a few telephone calls and arrange an appointment to sign up with another. In doing so losing any chance of working for the agency you're already with, but at least the wife will be happy that you can attend your daughters parents evening. However, it's a bit of a gamble because the next agency may assign you with the same client as the last one.

Many companies use multiple agencies, and your name will have been given to the awaiting assessor. Decision time, let the family down. After all, you need the money, and bills don't pay themselves. No, change of thought, you decide to let the assessor down because family comes first, and they already think you're unreliable as it is. But you need the money. Then your mind flits again. It doesn't matter because you hardly received any work anyway. Instead you please your wife because she can go out with her friends, your daughter is pleased because dad can take her to the parents evening, and for the first time show off her school.

In the morning you can sign up to another agency, praying they don't reassign you to the same company that offered an assessment at short notice that fuelled your erratic decision in the first place. And so the vicious circle of signing up to various driving agencies begins.

After many, many wasted enquiries you decide on an agency boasting that they have loads of work at prestigious blue-chip companies offering excellent opportunities. In doing so the seed of doubt about agency reliability planted by your first, second, third and fourth encounter springs to the forefront of your mind. And such acorn of doubt is destined to grow into a huge oak tree of resentment as you try other agencies, all promising the same, yet rarely delivered.

So you try another, then another, until one appears to offer a genuine assignment with good rates of pay and on-going work. You sign up, and wonders of wonders you're offered work in the guise of a text message: tomorrow 06:00 then for the rest of the week with the same start times. You're in.

Turning up early to give a good first impression, you enter the transport office full of strangers – full time drivers that resent agency drivers. As for the transport clerk, he or she hates you. Transport clerks don't know why they hate you because the complicated thought process conflicting with their two only brain cells needed to keep them upright, feel they should hate you simply because full time drivers do.

The long and lonely walk, which takes an age to complete, ends at a hatch with a knuckle-dragging clerk standing behind it. He or she sneers at your presence, quickly changing to a smirk, knowing he or she has been given the power to ban you from site, or at least recommend a ban, any time he or she wishes. Even make up a story to get you a ban simply because he or she doesn't like the way you dress or speak, or for many other reasons. And there is nothing you can say or do to defend yourself. He or she is right, and therefore you are guilty, without any investigation or reasoning.

All clerks long for the chance to say those three little words that are given to them to use like a perverted dictator passing sentence: 'banned from site.' Although they'd struggle to spell it. And when they hand you a clump of paperwork for you to, somehow, already understand, even though it's your first time to drive for them, they get a thrill answering your questions with sarcastic comments. Nothing too taxing, otherwise their remaining brain cell will have to compete with over-thought, which means having to sit down.

Be prepared to receive the dirtiest and usually the most knackered truck too. Be it a rigid or articulated vehicle, it may appear clean on the outside, but the inside will almost certainly be a disgrace and stink to high heaven. The transport clerk knows this, and will extract huge amounts of twisted fun handing you the keys. And if you are driving an artic, the trailer will also be a mess; guaranteed to have at least one fault that may result in points against your licence if pulled by the police or DVSA.

Full time drivers employed by the company, however, constantly moan and gripe about their vehicles. And I do mean their vehicles. Many full time drivers have a vehicle assigned to them, and it is their responsibility to take care of it; reporting the slightest of faults. But the same driver may have their truck used by an agency driver whilst taking their weekly rest or during holiday periods.

They do not like that at all, and will almost certainly blame agency drivers of any damage they previously committed to shroud their own incompetence. Guess who the transport manager will believe? After all, agency drivers are a dispensable commodity to exploit, poke fun, vent frustration and generally abuse.

In fairness, there is a minority of agency drivers that have little care about personal hygiene, let alone a tidy cab. Then again, the same can be said of a minority of full time drivers. But agency drivers are, unfortunately, tarred with the same brush, and it takes quite a considerable amount of time before one can be trusted. It is also true that full time driver's hate the fact agency drivers can earn more money than they do. True, to a certain extent, but full time drivers are guaranteed work and can return to the same job after holiday leave. Agency drivers are most definitely not.

Holiday pay is protected by law for full time, part time and yes, even agency workers, but never think you are safe from persecution. Agencies begrudge this law, simply because their drivers aren't earning any income for them. However, there is no law to keep an agency driver assigned to a particular company. In other words, taking a holiday can jeopardise any chance of returning to the same place. After all, the agency's client still needs a driver to cover holiday leave for his own drivers.

Agency drivers returning from holiday, however, will most likely find themselves assigned elsewhere and usually with a company that previous agency drivers turned down because the assignment conditions are horrific. So the answer is simple – don't have a holiday. But thanks to EU Working Time Directive, this is no longer an option.

All drivers now have to take leave if they see themselves exceeding their maximum 48-hours per week averaged over a 17-week period. In a way this directive has ended many assignments where agency drivers were happy to work. Only to be moved elsewhere because they had no choice but take a holiday so not to break any EU laws, then having to seek a further assignment suited to their needs and home life, often through seeking yet another agency, and the viscous circle starts again.

Chapter 10

THE FUTURE

21st Century trucks have come a long way since Wilhelm Maybach and his first internal combustion engine powered truck in 1896. Lucky for him an organisation called the EU was decades away from existence before it could interfere with truck design or development by introducing outrageous compulsory rules and regulations manufactures had no choice but to adhere.

According to the EU large trucks are a huge danger to health, and carbon emission levels produced by trucks are incredibly high. But the EU tend to be blissfully unaware that modern trucks create less emissions than many cars. This hatred of trucks seems to pollute their judgement of HGV technology, and that it is further developed than the car industry. In fact, it's the truck industry that developed better emission technology where car manufactures now use in their vehicles.

In the meantime EU bureaucrats carries on regardless with their loathing of trucks, as well as cars, dedicated, as they say, to improving road safety and driving that all important carbon footprint down, whatever the cost to any motorist. Unless you drive an all-electric car, that actually produces a larger carbon footprint in its construction before being placed in a showroom, compared to a ten-year old Land Rover Discovery.

The EU is also an expert at interfering with manufactures and their research and development projects, adamant that truck manufactures must concentrate on less emissions, better fuel consumption and curvier cabs. HGV manufactures continue development into bodywork design to reduce impact upon the drivers should collisions occur, larger windows and advanced mirrors to improve driver visibility and blind spots. And with technology advancement in curved cabs fuel costs could be reduced by a quarter, apparently.

The European Commission proposed yet more rules to force manufacturers develop better aerodynamic lorries, aimed to reduce fuel consumption, cut emissions of greenhouse gases, and also enhance the safety of vulnerable road users. In other words, yet more tougher regulations enforced by the EU to punish their nemesis, the HGV.

Former EU Vice-President Siim Kallas, responsible for transport, said: 'A brick is the least aerodynamic shape you can imagine. That is why we need to improve the shape of lorries on our roads. These changes make road transport cleaner and safer. They will reduce hauliers fuel bills and give European manufacturers a head-start in designing the truck of the future, a greener truck for the global market.'

The irony is, it was the EU that originally devised directives for truck manufactures having to design box-type HGV's in the first place to maximise load capacity. And when it came to exhaust emissions, according to the Department for Transport (DfT) Heavy Goods Vehicles on British roads contribute around only 20% of road transport greenhouse gasses. Meanwhile, Gary, Margaret and Malcolm contribute the remaining 80% but will never admit it.

The most significant emissions savings will come from the use of lower emission technologies such as hybrid, electric technologies and alternative fuels such as bio-methane and compressed natural gas used already by some bus and haulage companies. Both fuels, however, have a huge and expensive draw-back – decreasing the lifetime of modern diesel engines, exacerbate the delicate balance of precise fuel injection systems, increase further costs with servicing programmes and downtime. Something the DfT fails to incorporate in their studies.

The study also fails to recognise that a large percentage of foreign HGV's have increased ten-fold year-on-year since 1998 – coincidentally when UK rules, laws and regulations were naively signed over to the EU by the then Labour foreign Secretary, Jack Straw. And it's because of the large influx of foreign HGV's the DfT's findings are nowhere near accurate.

A simple solution to decrease the total truck emissions contribution was to increase the usage of home-based HGV's by collecting containers and trailers from ports, thus decreasing the amount of foreign vehicles on the road. But someone from the real world mentioned that the same trip would have still been made, regardless using a foreign truck or otherwise.

Electric power: Steam power had been used for transporting goods for over 100-years before the technology could be shrunk enough to fit small engines into cars and trucks. But again, distance and re-fuelling was an issue. The only other source of automotive propulsion left that could travel further and took only a few minutes to re-fuel was the internal combustion engine powered vehicle.

Fully electrically powered battery trucks are by no means a new concept. In 1914 General Motors developed and manufactured light rigid trucks in Detroit to deliver goods, including newspapers. Electric power had always been a means of propulsion of cars and light trucks during the early pioneers of internal combustion engine technology.

Even as far back as the First World War electric vehicles begun to outsell petrol power, where 28% of all cars in the USA were battery powered. Some of which covered a distance of 70-miles before the need of a recharge. And the reason why electric power failed to keep its remarkable lead on vehicle propulsion was simply down to battery life and recharge time.

Automotive manufacturers continue to put up with relentless nagging from governments determined to be better than their political counterpart by enforcing outrageous and often impossible clean air targets upon them. The first, and only viable response as far as I'm concerned, was, and still is, the hydrogen-cell fuelled engine, exhausting gases into the atmosphere consisting of nothing more than water.

But the cost to produce hydrogen-powered vehicles, as well as extracting hydrogen from water to fuel them, is astronomical. So as it stands we're left with the interim option, the Betamax of next generation power – all-electric vehicles, including cars, buses, trucks, trains and maybe one day, passenger-carrying aeroplanes. But to make and produce the millions of green, polar bear friendly, battery-powered vehicles is a colossal drain on resources and the environment on a global scale.

Batteries that power electric cars are set to increase by enormous proportions, and by 2025 will engulf 90 percent of all Lithium-ion battery production. From its raw material state to end production, this 'so called' environmentally friendly automotive alternative actually produces twice as much carbon footprint than conventional internal combustion engines. Let me explain.

From mining of raw materials, they travel around the world to battery manufactures, only to travel back around the world a second time to car manufactures, remarkably travelling around the world yet again to car distributors. And this is before a single turn of an end users brand new wheel. The new owner then has to keep recharging the battery, where more often than not, the electricity used to charge it will come from a fossil fuelled or nuclear powered station.

To add a further problem the UK alone produces only 5% excess electricity before any influx of battery powered vehicles taking over internal combustion power. And the USA actually produces a deficit of 14% electricity [2021] so has to import more power from elsewhere in the form of fossil fuels.

Ah, but if all power stations produced green energy then surely the carbon footprint to produce and run electric cars will eventually off-set conventional vehicles, I hear you say. Well no, not really. Firstly, there is simply nowhere near enough solar, wind, hydro-electric, renewable or even nuclear fuelled power stations on the planet to produce enough fossil fuel energy for other uses, let alone recharge battery powered vehicles.

Secondly, should all vehicles be miraculously replaced with battery power tomorrow, the amount of CO_2 poured into the atmosphere would send Millennials and Jeremy Vine into a frenzied panic. And forget garbage-fuelled DMC DeLorean cars, even with Doc's capabilities going back to the future.

Thirdly, and to rub battery acid into the environmentally friendly activist wound, on paper it will take 9 or 10-years for a battery powered car to off-set any carbon footprint. But this falls into insignificance due to the fact car batteries only has around a 7-year life cycle, so a replacement is required. And because batteries that power car motors cannot be fully recycled [2021] the replacement battery will have to be a new one. And the manufacturing cycle from raw material to end product begins all over again.

To add another conveniently brushed under the carpet problem, most new cars are replaced within 4 or 5-years, especially by the largest end user – fleet markets. And should a recycled system miraculously appear out of thin air, it wouldn't be needed due to demand for replacement new cars, where, yes you've guessed it, and the entire manufacturing process begins again.

Only this time a used un-recyclable battery mountain of huge proportion will quickly appear by 2025, leaving the industry to store around 10,000,000 tonnes, or over 50,000,000 inefficient, environmentally damaging, soil polluting, fluffy squirrel killing Lithium-ion batteries. And that's not including the extra electricity drained from fossil-fuelled power stations for charging them at least twice on a daily basis.

Boat and yacht builders, plant and agricultural machinery, not forgetting HGV manufacturers are developing fully electric vehicles, including tractor units to haul 44-tonnes of goods in 50-feet trailers up and down motorways. Doubling the size of an unregulated growing knackered battery mountain with quadruple sized batteries weighing in excess of 4-tonnes. And these colossal industrial batteries create larger mines for the considerably larger quantities of raw materials, a huge demand on fossil-fuelled energy to extract it and increasing pollution to produce them.

In 2015 Cobalt – one of many materials used to make Lithium-ion batteries – rose considerably in value within 12-months by a staggering 80%. And in 2020 almost 200,000 tonnes of this precious material was processed and shipped to manufactures, inevitably increasing the cost, where, as always, paid for by the end user. Then there is Lithium; a rarer material than Cobalt, yet just as important towards the manufacturing of these 'so called' environmentally friendly batteries. And by 2025 almost 800,000 tonnes will be mined to keep up with demand, where it takes 1,000 tonnes of ore to extract only one tonne of Lithium.

Further materials such as Chromium, Copper, Graphite and Nickel are also needed. Mined in Russia, the Philippines, Indonesia, China, Australia and Canada. One mine in Australia alone produces 100,000 tonnes of Nickel Sulphate per year, generating incredible toxic issues for the environment. Spewing tonnes of harmful gases and dust clouds into the atmosphere, as well as sulphuric acid and other oxidised Nickel waste into nearby rivers and streams, turning them red and killing wild life. Respiratory and cancer illnesses, child deformities and premature deaths are a contributing factor of living near these dangerous areas, and are on the increase.

Graphite is predominately mined in China, where strict regulations on air and water pollution are a tad different in some other countries, such as Canada and Australia. Pollution from mining and processing Graphite has caused local health issues and damaged surrounding crops by poisoning the soil. Combining all materials and its processing to extract these precious metals from ores has created an outrageously devastating environmental impact. Add the destruction of land and the stripping of forests covering thousands of acres, the green solution to create a cleaner environment is seemingly tarnished somewhat. But surely the sacrifice is worth it?

Those employed by mines from poorer countries suffer worse health problems, where it seems employers have mislaid the memo on Health and Safety. Thousands of incredibly low paid labourers are treated no different from those during the industrial revolution. That includes incredibly long shifts, working 6 and even 7-days per week, and using child labour. And let's not forget powering the enormous energy used to extract and process these precious metals are mainly sourced from coal fuelled power stations. Still want an electric car?

21st Century fully electric trucks are still nowhere near being a viable productive tool in road haulage. Nissan, and its New Electric Cabstar, claims it to be a favourite vehicle choice for so many businesses. And a vocational licence isn't required to drive the electric Cabstar due to the payload being only one metric tonne, with a top speed of 25-mph and a maximum range of 45-miles. That may be the case for some businesses with only town and city deliveries of light goods, but for the average operator of small HGV's electric power has a little more to go to prove its haulage capability.

So motorways are out of the question, including dual carriageways, at least for the time being. But in fairness to Nissan, at least they're having a go at being one of the first to jump in the deep ocean of uncertainty when it comes to electrically-powered load carrying vehicles. Battery powered HGV's are obviously a long way off superseding diesel power. Or are they?

An average weight of around 7-tonnes for a tractor unit would have to be doubled with a similar weight of batteries to pull a 44-tonne load. But the extra battery weight would decrease the legal maximum load of a trailer, not to mention a huge compromise on speed and range between recharge. However, Mercedes-Benz, DAF, Scania, Volvo and other truck manufactures continue to develop their own next-generation battery powered trucks, pouring millions of Euros into research.

One recharging and propulsion solution is to electrify stretches of motorways with overhead power cables – not unlike railway and tramway electric cables – recharging batteries in large trucks as they drive. Trials have already taken place through joint manufacturer efforts in Sweden, Germany and the UK, where the UK government injected £20 million in 2020 for further development of this technology.

In 2017 Sweden electrified part of its E16 motorway, outside the city of Gavle. Scania, with their overhead powered prototype truck, operated live tests amongst other road users. When it came to the end of the road, so to speak, the truck then returns to being either fully electric or a hybrid, driving whilst charging the batteries not just from overhead cables, but also its euro-6 diesel engine running on diesel or bio-fuel.

After years of talks, meetings and co-operation between the government and private businesses, the 2-kilometre section uses technology developed by electrical giants, Siemens. Claes Erixon, head of Scania Research & Development, believes this technology is one important milestone on the journey towards fossil-free transport. But what kind of fuel powered the cables? Whatever, the electric road is a key component in achieving Sweden's ambition of an energy-efficient and fossil-free vehicle fleet by 2030. Yeah, right.

The electric road is one of many pioneering technologies being developed as an alternative to fossil fuel powered vehicles. They are also combining these technologies with their experimental autonomous vehicles. It's a crying shame the UK no longer has any truck manufacturers left to further develop electric trucks and stay ahead of the rest in truck innovation as we once did. But we can save some face, as many of the technology, hardware and software, has been invented, developed and even manufactured in the UK so foreign companies with wads of cash may exploit our still brilliant engineering capabilities.

Gottlieb Daimler and Wilhelm Maybach would be totally bemused by the new Mercedes battery-powered truck. Starting a limited production in 2017 the Mercedes eTruck is a fully battery powered commercial HGV used for delivering goods around towns and cities, with a maximum range of around 124 miles. The truck has three lithium-ion batteries sitting inside the length of the vehicle's chassis, with room for further batteries to extend the range. The vehicle is also fitted with all-round cameras where images are displayed on a screen fitted within the driver's view.

A digital instrument display on the dashboard provided vehicle information and a SatNav with the trucks route for the driver, including three modes of drive: automatic, economical and agile – more power. There is a constant monitoring of the vehicle's movement, route, battery power, cargo space and weight, where warnings of distance and battery levels are relayed to the driver to ensure the truck reaches its destination in the safest, most efficient and economical way. And should the driver be encouraged to rush a little by putting a strain on the battery, the truck will automatically switch to 'Achtung! I'm in charge mode' and decide for itself a suitable mode to get to its destination.

A handheld tablet issued to the driver gives the same sensor readings as the dash of the truck, including battery life and mileage left under relevant driving and cargo conditions. And with a load capacity of a possible 26-tonnes it certainly paves the way towards battery powered HGV's, apparently. But for now the truck won't be sold to any potential customers. In the meantime Daimler launched a limited production of the eCanter in New York, Lisbon and Tokyo, also in 2017. Although having a limited range at only 62-miles, it is quite smaller than the Mercedes all-electric HGV. It boils down to battery technology in the end, which is coming on leaps and bounds.

But any government ambition to meet a Net-Zero carbon emission plan by 2050 is nothing but a pipe dream. The technology, financial infrastructure and road development is simply not there. Let's be honest, it took the

High Ways department over 2 years to construct a single round-a-bout in Corby, Northamptonshire. A decade to upgrade – not build from scratch – but upgrade stretches of the M1 motorway. So to modernise the entire motorway network to carry over-head power cables in 30- years is impossible.

As mentioned before, all this electrification malarkey is the Betamax before hydrogen-power or biogas takes the helm. Even today [2021] bin lorries are collecting refuse in Gothenburg, Sweden, fuelled by hydrogen. The trucks are cleaner, quieter and the only emissions exhausted to atmosphere is water.

Scania sees hydrogen fuel cell technology as a complement to battery-electric vehicles. Even Biogas is making its mark between Scania, mobility provider Flixbus and gas supplier Gasum. The first long distance coach running on biogas is set to start operation between Stockholm and Oslo. Powered by liquid biogas (LBG) the coaches will reduce climate impact compared to fossil fuels.

Biogas is currently used in compressed form in a number of buses, cars and light commercial vehicles. Even some HGV's have trialed this type of fuel, including hauliers in the UK. And biogas is not only a fuel with the lowest CO_2 emission, it's fossil-free, renewable, reduces users CO_2 footprint anything up to 90% with air quality improvements. It is only in recent years that technology has been developed to cool biogas down to minus 160 degrees Celsius so that it becomes liquid and usable as a fuel. In doing so biogas can not only be used for cars, light and heavy commercials applications, but also plant, generators and marine engines.

Availability of biogas can vastly improve throughout Europe, especially as the EU has already making fuelling stations along main European road networks, where 17% of Europe's vehicle gas grid is supplied with liquid biogas [2021]. In Sweden it is at 95% [2021], both dramatically cutting CO2 emissions. And half of the EU's HGV's could be fuelled by biogas by 2025. One downside, it can totally knacker your fuel injection system if not properly maintained.

Autonomous driverless trucks: Of course, electric battery power runs alongside the inevitable driverless vehicle. Well, it is almost upon us, battery powered or not. And some truck manufactures, including Mercedes, Volvo and Scania, have been developing and testing prototypes, aiming to make them commercially viable. A surprise pioneer in this automotive field of technology is Google, where they started to develop an autonomous car in 2009. Incredibly, the car completed trials of 100,000 miles on public roads without other road users even knowing.

By the summer 2015 driverless cars could be on British roads. Well, according to former Liberal Democrat Business Secretary, Vince Cable. Of course, he wasn't just wrong, he was amazingly incredibly premature with his outrageous statement. He continued to say: 'the excellence of our scientists and engineers has established the UK as pioneers in the development of driverless vehicles through pilot projects... 'today's announcement [January 2015] will see driverless cars take to our streets in less than six months, putting us at the forefront of this transformational technology and opening up new opportunities for our economy and society.'

A huge supporter of autonomous vehicles, former Transport Minister, Claire Perry, said: 'driverless cars have huge potential to transform the UK's transport network. They could improve safety, reduce congestion and lower emissions, particularly CO2... 'we are determined to ensure driverless cars can fulfil this potential which is why we are actively reviewing regulatory obstacles to create the right framework to trial these vehicles on British roads.'

The UK coalition government allowed the first trials of computer-controlled cars to start in January 2015 as part of a move to update the law and allow driverless cars on public roads. But Ministers admitted that the current Highway Code and British roads are inadequate for a driverless vehicle. And these Johnny cabs (reference to the film Total Recall) operates by using GPS technology to locate the vehicle's position on an electronic map.

Google unveiled its computerised 'hands-free' self-driving bubble car in June 2014 that has no steering wheel, brake or accelerator pedals. Instead, it has buttons for start, pull over and emergency stop, and a computer screen showing the planned route. That's it.

In Japan Nissan successfully carried out its first public road test of a driverless car by using its 'Leaf' electric vehicle on a highway South West of Tokyo in November 2014. Carlos Ghosn, the chief executive of Nissan, said that innovations to ease congestion and emissions are badly needed due to the increasing number of global cities. Nissan is making progress on an autonomous car in both Japan and France, where the French government authorised testing with a view to opening roads to autonomous vehicles by 2020.

The Japanese carmaker has also been working with universities including MIT, Stanford and Oxford. It says around 90% of road accidents are currently caused by human error. Actually it's closer to 95% depending on where statistics are collated. Under Nissan's system, drivers remain at the wheel but the vehicle can automatically steer, brake, accelerate, change lanes, merge into traffic and maintain a safe distance from other vehicles.

Computerised HGV convoys controlled by just one driver have already been tested on British roads. The trucks are electronically linked together, where the driver of the front vehicle controls the acceleration, braking and steering of the others within the vehicle pack, allowing a road train to travel long distances on motorways with only a few yards between each vehicle.

Whilst the other HGV's in line would still have dedicated drivers, the automated system would allow them to 'switch off' for most of the journey. In an emergency, or at busy junctions, the drivers following the lead trucks will be able to retake control of their vehicles. Backers of the proposal, including the EU, say the system will allow drivers to use their laptop, read a book or sit back and enjoy a relaxed lunch. And fuel
consumption may be cut by 10%. Really? I predict the truck driver will still be a target for blame, even when he isn't.

Fuel efficiency of a road train will be achieved by decreasing aerodynamic drag whilst in a tight streamline formation. The vehicles would communicate via Wi-Fi, so that if the lead vehicle changes speed, the others follow suit. In addition the movement of the entire convoy will be monitored by laser sensors and infrared cameras. Experts of the new technology say businesses will benefit in a multitude of ways. Whether they are waiting for delivery of goods or executives to arrive for meetings, smoother traffic flow will make journey times more predictable and scheduling simple.

Driver or operator of the vehicle can carry out other tasks while travelling and arrive at their destination fresher. In Europe 76% of total goods traffic in 2011 were transported by road, according to the European Union. Once again, these experts and the EU fail to recognise that it is 99.9% of goods are delivered by road – be it by a HGV or a small 1-ton van.

European, and most certainly UK roads, are becoming increasingly congested whilst major road networks have hardly expanded in comparison since the 1970's. Yet the manufacture of cars and HGV's traffic is set to substantially explode in numbers over the next decade or so. Mercedes trucks is in the process of developing their HGV's and the 'Truck 2025' with the promise that in a decade HGV drivers will become 'transport managers' rather than truck drivers. That, of course, is impossible due to the fact transport managers are yet to discover that crayons are used for colouring pictures, not for eating. So drivers are simply too intelligent to be transport managers.

According to Mercedes trucks their autonomous vehicles, once driving at around 50 mph on a highway, the driver will be prompted to activate the Highway Pilot placing the truck in autonomous mode, leaving the driver free to pivot the seat 45 degrees. The driver will then have access to a centre console enabling them to use a removable touch-screen computer to complete other tasks. Again, really? A blameless driver?

Of course, the introduction of driverless HGV's will have to meet and try to overcome considerable legal obstacles. An amendment to the UN Convention on Road Traffic was agreed to allow a car to drive itself so long as the driver is present and able to override the automated system if necessary. This means still putting the driver at blame of any incident.

One company that has already built fully autonomous trucks is Peloton Technology, based in Silicon Valley, California, USA. It is a system that could immediately save lives, save money and reduce fuel costs. The haulage business is massive across the EU, keeping all of its member States fluid in commerce and industry. There are over 400,000 miles of roadways in the UK alone. And in Europe, including the UK, there are approximately 6.5 million HGV's on the road at any given time. 35 million in the USA, and a staggering 350 million in China [2021].

The term peloton is working on the principle of competitive cycling where riders cluster in a group – the peloton – to catch the least wind resistance. This principle applies to a truck convoy where upon a leading truck allows a trailing truck to exploit wind resistance and therefore produce a better fuel consumption. The leading truck also benefits by decreasing its effect against turbulence left in a HGV's passing, or wake, considerably effecting its aerodynamics.

Peloton technology developed a system that allows two HGV's to follow each other far more closely to each other (platooning) than humanly possible without prosecution for tailgating. There is no physical link between the trucks, travelling between 23 and 6-metres apart, compared to a human distance of 50 - 100 metres or so, depending upon speed and road conditions to allow for reaction times.

Platooning by autonomous trucks claims a saving of up to, yet again, that amazing total of 10% in fuel costs for the rear truck and 4.5% for the lead truck. And fuel costs for haulage companies account for around 40% of the business, if not more in some cases. But these fuel savings using diesel power are purely academic as autonomous vehicles future lies with battery power only, according to EU governments.

Nevertheless, in tests, the rear vehicle has a computer screen to show the driver what the front vehicle can see on the road ahead. The front truck also has a screen so the view of the rear truck can be seen by the driver - in effect acting like a rear view mirror. The view also displays driver blind spots. The front truck communicates directly with the rear truck, conveying information including braking, vehicle speed and engine torque, taking only a flick of a switch to engage the system. The rear driver still has to concentrate, though, and continue to control steering, but the brakes and accelerator are handed over to the computer.

The system isn't entirely autonomous, but it's a step in the right direction. And Peloton Technology isn't alone producing such systems. Satre (Safe Road Trains for the Environment) completed tests on trucks and Volvo cars driving in formation at distances of just 4-metres apart. But such a tight distance conflicts with laws, rules and regulations, coupled with technological and moral issues. Yet the UK government, bullied by the EU, are both hell-bent pursuing this technology, regardless of any conflicting issues on tracks, as well as public roads.

First of all, and as us night drivers already know, driving through the night on Britain's motorways and dual carriageways are still incredibly busy, mainly with HGV's. And the morning rush hour is starting earlier and earlier each year, at the moment around 4am. Gone are the days passing the odd HGV or car in the early hours. I for one can confidently say there is only a slight respite in HGV traffic during the night. No, hang on, I've changed my mind. There isn't any respite. I forgot to mention the amount of road works, diversions, speed restrictions and closed junctions.

Putting aside long term major repairs or developments up and down the country, the majority of lane and junction closures, even entire road sections are closed at night. Sometimes earlier and longer than planned or expected, or even without any warning at all.

Detours set in place, which always appear somewhere along trunk routes 24/7 365-days a year, will simply not accommodate fully autonomous vehicle, let alone HGV's. Low bridges, tight roads through towns and even villages, parked cars and the ability to turn around or seek an alternative route will have to be negotiated, putting an organic driver back in the autonomous driving seat.

So there is very much a necessity for a driver to occupy the cab and most likely having to take control to deliver that important load, rendering the technology useless and a waste of money for the operator. It is evident that cars and HGV's are a considerably long way off being totally driverless, no matter how much the EU and British government paint their pretty picture of autonomous vehicles.

Distribution centres, warehouses and stores, in particular their loading bays will cause huge headaches for any computer whiz-kid thinking they can develop a system for trucks to reverse into position – having to negotiate badly placed pallets, to name one hazard – without the use of a driver. Many truck drivers will agree that not all deliveries are made to new spacious warehouses and distribution centres. Most are old and inadequate for articulated trucks. Even so, new or old, there are numerous obstacles to overcome.

Adverse weather conditions are also a major concern. It's all very well trucks and trailers having ABS and TEBS fitted to control the vehicle from going into a skid, but modern safety systems don't know what snow or ice looks like. Only a professional driver has a better feel to negotiate such difficult conditions, then react accordingly by naturally trying to correct the vehicle or avoid other road users, pedestrians and buildings. Not forgetting enormous potholes and soft road edges. Sudden downpours are another factor to take into consideration when it comes to having to make emergency manoeuvres.

Following a convoy of driverless HGV's creates other road safety issues. Inevitably it will be difficult for road users to read road signs when stuck behind a road train. A complete re-design of all road signs will have to be implemented. And during traffic standstill a queue can easily continue a mile away from the junction, making exit and entry very difficult as platooned road trains and its on-board systems won't allow the convoy to be separated. So bad news for Audi drivers. In turn, traffic light systems, road works and accidents will also upset a convoy of driverless trucks.

Attitude of non-vocational drivers will have to be taken into consideration. In the UK it is not necessary for learner drivers of cars to be aware of HGV's and how they negotiate roads, junctions and traffic islands. So what chance do they have against a driverless HGV negotiating a round-a-bout on a dual carriageway only to try, as car drivers do, cut up the near side of an HGV not realising that an articulated truck bends.

Autonomous trucks will then only come to an immediate halt to minimise any possibility of a collision, and stay where it is until the hazard has passed. But the car driver will undoubtedly refuse to get out of the way, so at least an organic driver can move and let traffic flow before he kicks the shit of Malcolm.

The obvious happens only far too often, and of course, it is never the car driver's fault. It has to be the truck driver because he has no care about other road users, according to other road users. But how can a car driver blame a driverless truck? Who is to blame? So maybe it is time a car test included the awareness of HGV's. Chew on that Malcolm.

What would Boris Johnson think of the autonomous HGV's? After all, he won't be able to make the truck go on a cycle awareness program. And more to the point, driverless trucks will not deviate from restrictions or the Highway Code, forcing cyclists to obey the rules because, as far as the truck and its computer system is concerned, isn't making or about to make a driving mistake, thus broken any rules or laws. But, but, but, cyclists are never wrong. They always obey all rules, so truck computers must be wrong.

When a cyclist makes a mistake by cutting – no sorry, I mean when a truck gets in the way of a cyclist – the result tends to be a tad squishy and death will most probably follow, if not serious injury. However, the first death of a cyclist will certainly place the government in a quandary: ban driverless trucks or cyclists. Given the choice I know which one I'd choose. As for truck drivers, I think the vocation is safe, at least for the time being. Doesn't mean your particular job is safe, though.

Agency drivers, for instance, could easily become a thing of the past, simply because haulage companies and operators will no longer need the service of an agency. So the closure of driving agencies will certainly be a real threat. Oh dear, how sad, never mind. And judging by the EU track record against truck drivers, no doubt an extra truck category will be added to an already crowded licence. Not forgetting extra cost having to pass yet another qualification and carry yet another card to prove they're qualified to operate an autonomous vehicle. Maybe a diploma or even a degree in navigation and computer electronics will be required instead of a driving licence.

When it comes to an accident, who is to blame? And what about drink driving laws. Can an operator of a driverless vehicle involved in an accident be lawfully breathalised whilst the vehicle was driving itself? Common sense says yes, of course. After all, an operator will need to be in charge of the vehicle at all times, and will also be needed to negotiate stores, distribution centres and loading bays, won't they? So surely that means existing EU WTD and UK driving regulations will apply? Many questions still need answering.

Law-lords will be cursing each other trying to find some kind of concrete foundation to support existing laws covering various Road Traffic Regulations, if not to save time. But it only takes a bright lawyer to find cracks and loopholes that will inevitably appear if or when these vehicles hit the road and accidents start to pile up, so to speak.

Consultations with the Department for Transport may help to clear up the ethical conundrum of whether man or machine is responsible for accidents. And if the technology is to realise its full potential, large numbers of driverless vehicles must be able to communicate with each other faultlessly, as well as be aware of other road users. One thing is for sure there are many laws, rules, regulations, technology reliability, capability and other factors to consider. So maybe the golden era for HGV's is yet to come.

Still want to be a lorry driver?

KEEP ON TRUCKIN'

GLOSSARY

ABS... Advance Braking System
AEC... Associated Equipment Company
ANPR... Automatic Number Plate Recognition
API... American Petroleum Institute
ATF... Authorised Testing Facility
AWD... All Wheel Drive

BHP... Brake Horse Power
BMC... British Motor Corporation
BMW... Bayerische Motoren Werke
BRS... British Road Services
BST... British Summer Time

CARB... California Air Resources Board
CB... Citizen Band (radio)
CI... Compression Ignition
CP... Common Parts
CPC... Certificate of Professional Competence
CMPG... Central Motorway Police Group
CO2... Carbon Dioxide

DAF... Doorne's Automobiel Fabriek (Van Doorne's Automobile Factory)
DCPC... Drivers Certificate of Professional Competence
DFT... Department for Transport
Digi-card... Digital tachograph drivers (smart) card

DP... Designated Premises
DPF... Diesel particulate Filter
DR... Drink Driving (offence)
DSA... Driving Standards Agency
DTCs... Deputy Traffic Commissioner(s)
DVSA... Driver and Vehicle Standards Agency

EBS... Electronic Braking System
ECU... Electronic Control Unit
EKA... EKA Ltd. (Rotzler (UK) ltd.)
ENASA... Empresa Nacional de Autocamiones (S.A)
EPA... United States Environmental Protection Agency
ERF... Edwin Richard Foden
EU... European Union

FM... Frequency Modification
FORS... Freight Operators Recognition Scheme

GATSO... Gatsometer (BV)
GMT... Greenwich Mean Time
GP... General Purpose
GPS... Global Position System
GV79... Good Vehicle (issue 79)
GVTS ... Goods vehicle testing station
GVW... Gross Vehicle Weight

HGV... Heavy Goods Vehicle
HP... Horse Power
Hi-Viz... High Visibility
HMRC... Her Majesty's Revenue and Customs
HQ... High Cube

IN... No Insurance (offence)
ISBU... Intermodal Steel Building Unit
ISO... International Shipping Organisation
IVECO... Industrial Vehicles Corporation

JAUPT... Joint Approvals Unit Periodic Training

KPH... Kilometres Per Hour
Kw... KiloWatt (power output measurement)

lb... Pound (imperial weight measure)
LGV... Large Goods Vehicle
Ltr... Litre

MAM... Maximum Authorised Mass
MAN... Maschinenfabrik Augsburg-Nürnberg
Mhz... Megahertz (radio airwave frequency)
MIT... Massachusetts Institute of Technology
MOT... Ministry of Transport
MP... Member of Parliament
MPG... Miles Per Gallon
MPH... Miles Per Hour

NACCO... North American Coal Corporation
NHS... National Health Service
NI... National Insurance
NOX... Nitrogen Oxide (sensor)

OCR... Oxford, Cambridge and Royal Society (of Arts Examinations Board)
OSCAR... One Step Cab Access
OSA... Obstructive Sleep Apnoea

PACCAR... Pacific Car (and Foundry Company)
PAYE... Pay As You Earn
PCV... Positive Crankcase Ventilation
PI... Public Inquiry
POA... Period Of Availability
PSV... Passenger Service Vehicle

RA... Royal Artillery
RASC... Royal Army Service Corps
REME... Royal Electrical Mechanical Engineers
Road Trains for the Environment
RSL... Road Speed Limiter
RTR... Royal Tank Regiment

Sat Nav... Satellite Navigation
Satre... Safe road Trains for the Environment
SPECS... Speed Check Services
SVDD... Support Vector Data Description

TAN... Traffic Area Network
TAO... Traffic Area Office
TEBS Trailer Electronic Braking System
TEW... Twenty-Foot (containers)
TVW... Transport Vehicles Warrington

UK... United Kingdom
UN... United Nations
US... United States
USA... United States of America
UTC... Universal Time Coordinated

VASCAR... Visual Average Speed Computer And Recorder
VAT... Valued Added Tax
VGT6... Vehicle Goods Type 6 (Ministry test plate)
VI... Vehicle Inspectorate
VOSA... Vehicle and Operator Services Agency
VU... Vehicle Unit

WABCO... Westinghouse Air Brake Company
Wi-Fi... a play on the audiophile term Hi-Fi. The Wi-Fi
Alliance defines Wi-Fi as any Wireless Local Area Network
WiMS... Weigh in Motion Sensors
WTD... Working Time Directive

ZF... Zahnradfabrik (Gearbox manufacture) Factory

Bring back Foden!

So you want to be a lorry driver

Printed in Great Britain
by Amazon